UP&
FWD

30 Day Devotional

Dwight Follins

Rackhouse Publishing
Read to Learn, Write to Remember

Copyright © 2020 Dwight Follins
All rights reserved. No part of this manuscript may be reproduced, stored in a retrieval system or transmitted in any form, or by any means, electronic, mechanical, photocopying, recording or otherwise, without prior permission of the author.

Scripture quotations are taken from the Holy Bible, New International Version®, NIV®. Copyright ©1973,1978,1984,2011 By Biblica, Inc. New King James Version®. Copyright © 1982 by Thomas Nelson. Used by permission. All rights reserved.

ISBN-13: 978-1-7355350-3-6

For information about custom editions, special sales, premium and bulk purchases, please contact:
WWW.DWIGHTFOLLINS.COM

First Edition
Printed in the U.S.A

Up & Forward: 30 Day Devotional

DEDICATION

This devotional is dedicated to those who have transitioned from earth to glory and are now living in eternal rest and victory. For we are indeed surrounded by a cloud of witnesses (Hebrews 12:1). I dedicate this book to those who, before leaving this earth, imparted impactful wisdom into me that I will never forget. I miss you all dearly, Ernest L Pender (daddy), Dontavious Boatwright, Bishop Kenneth Moles Sr., Bishop James E Paris Sr. & Mother Isabel Paris, Mother Margaret Annis, Pastor Nathan L. Simmons, Apostle Donald Taylor, Dr. Kenneth McKnight, Robert Garrison, and my two amazing grandmothers, Dorothy Henry and Mabel Pender.

30 DAY DEVOTIONAL

CONTENTS

2
MENTALLY

Day 1: Break the Shell
Day 2: Essential Needs
Day 3: You're Able
Day4: Needful Mindfulness
Day 5: Transformers
Day6: Musical Medication

26
EMOTIONALLY

Day 7: Feelings are Not Facts
Day 8: Emotional Enemy
Day 9: Altered Anger
Day 10: Fruit Filled
Day 11: Almost
Day 12: Just Do it

44
SPIRITUALLY

Day 13: The Struggle is Real
Day 14: Command, Control, Create
Day 15: The Odds are in your Favor
Day 16: An Unbelievable Answer
Day 17 It's Not What it Looks Like
Day 18: Storm 101

64
PHYSICALLY

Day 19: Self-Care
Day 20: Get Uncomfortable
Day 21: Do Something
Day 22: Ability
Day 23: Rest & Relief
Day 24: Eat to Live

82
FINANCIALLY

Day 25: Sell, Pay, Live
Day 26: The Mouth & The Money
Day 27: Don't give up too Soon
Day 28: The Power of Process
Day 29: How to Deal with Dirty People
Day 30: Finances, Favor & Good Health

ACKNOWLEDGMENTS

Thanks be to God who gives us the victory and causes us to Triumph (2Corinthians 2:14).

I am indeed humbled to have an awesome little sister and publisher; thank you Melynda Rackley for pushing me to be bigger, better, and greater.

To my Noonday prayer Warrior family- you all have added so much wealth to my life. Thank you dearly for your love and support. As we say daily in noonday prayer, "Prayer is working and the righteous are winning."

Thank you momma, Pastor Betty Young and, H.E.R. amazing husband Freddie Young: for your loving support and raising me in the way of the Lord, love ya dearly.

To Bishop Dorothy Everett, Bishop Donna McCollors, Alexander Temple Community Church, Bishop Edward Robinson, and Lady Cynthia Robinson (Southside Church of God In Christ), Bishop Troy A. Bronner (Elim Christian Fellowship), Bishop Anthony Gilyard (Bethlehem Judah), Bishop Q S Caldwell (Joy Temple COP) and Dr. Dorinda Clark-Cole: words can not express how you all have positively impacted my life and ministry. Thank you for providing me with strong shoulders to lean on. God never ceases to amaze me. I'm so grateful that He gave me charge and gifted me to host prayer clinics in Atlanta GA, Philadelphia PA, and Jacksonville FL. My prayer clinic families are amazing: may God's power and presence continue to meet us in every service.

A really big thank you to the wind beneath my wings, the people that help me fly high: I love you dearly Ernesco and Tonya Pender (the world's greatest brother and sister-in love), Reginald Bernard Hardly (my brother like no other), Robin Brooks (the world's greatest best friend), Derick Scantling (simply the greatest), Tabitha Robinson (my counselor), Wanda Patterson (big Sis), Calvin Kraft (my personal motivator), Elder James Tillman (my mentor), and Dr. Deonia Simmons, (my Johnathan). I have found it to be true that if you surround yourself with people who empower you, believe in you, support you, lift you, motivate you, and appreciate you, good success will be your portion.

MENTALLY

A recent study on mental health disorders by John Hopkins University (hopkinsmedicine.org) revealed some interesting statistics. It stated that mental health disorders account for several of the top causes of disability in the US and world wide. These disorders include clinical depression, bipolar disorder, schizophrenia and obsessive-compulsive disorder. The study also revealed an estimated 26% of Americans, ages 18 and older (about 1 in 4 adults), suffer from a diagnosable mental disorder in a given year. Life is filled with unexpected surprises. These unexpected surprises help shape and mold not only our character, but also our mental wellness, thoughts, and habits. We are familiar with IQ, which is the intelligence quotient of a person; we are also familiar with EQ emotional intelligence (or quotient). However, we often forget about AQ (adaptability quotient) which is the ability to adapt. It is AQ which causes us to be able to absorb or adapt new information and new situations to determine our outcome. We use AQ to overcome struggles and move forward in life. AQ, along with God Conscience, is what gives us the momentum to move up and forward, or, stay still and stagnant. Proverbs 3:5: " trust in the Lord with all your heart; and lean not unto your own understanding. in all thy ways acknowledge him, and he shall direct your paths.." is one of the most frequently quoted scriptures in the Bible. This scripture comes alive when we don't just quote it, but actually do it. It helps us to adjust and adapt to life's uncertainties. Most people who choose to stay still and ruminate on a negative experience, or a dark part of their life, usually end up sad and experiencing one of the several mental disorders previously discussed (such as depression). Those who choose to use the negative experience as fuel and momentum for change often have more positive outcomes and outlooks on life. Prayer activates positive momentum: "The prayer of a righteous man is powerful and effective…(James 5:16). Momentum is force or speed of movement. It can also be strength of force gained by motion, or a series of events. Speed alone does not determine momentum; mass and speed are the governing factors of momentum. Emotionally, when a person takes a negative experience and uses it for positive reinforcement or energy, it becomes the mass or the weight of their influence to want better, to do better, and to live better. Positive momentum can also be contagious. Surrounding one's self with other people who are survivors, or who have overcome adverse circumstances, can be a positive influence. It can also add mass and movement to a person's experience during difficult times. The greater your destiny, future, or goals are, the harder and heavier your obstacles will be. That's because greater momentum means a larger amount of force will have to be used to stop an object or a person from moving. For the next six days, we will be focusing on positive factors of mental momentum that enhance adaptability and emotional mobility. These factors will cause us to continue to move up and forward to achieve emotional success and mental peace. "...and the peace of God which transcends all understanding will guard your hearts and your minds in Christ Jesus.." (Philippians 4:7)

Day 1
Break the shell

One Saturday morning, I was lying in bed, looking at the ceiling and pondering all the things I needed to do, but continuing, in my appeal, to be lazy. My phone began to alert me of new emails. As I opened some and deleted a few others, one in particular caught my attention. My sister sent me an awesome email about the symbolism of the willow tree. As I read about this amazing tree and its capability as one of the few trees which can bend into outrageous poses without snapping, one word began to stand out to me the most; "adaptability." The writing stated that because of adaptability, the willow somehow adjusts with life, rather than fighting it. It also shows how the tree continues to thrive, even in life's most challenging conditions. I then began to think to myself: if a tree has the ability to adjust, thrive, and live through strange and adverse conditions, then surely, so can I. "... not that I am speaking of being in need, for I have learned in whatever situation I am to be content. I know how to be brought low, and I know how to abound in every and any circumstance, I have learned the secret of facing plenty and hunger, abundance and need. I can do all things through him who strengthens me..." (Philippians 4:11-13 ESV).

After reading about the willow tree, I began to recall and remember so many things in my life I had to go through AND grow through. Just like the willow tree, I realized how adjustability not only sustained me, but advanced me. I remembered during the time of my sister's stroke, they rushed us via ambulance to another hospital in another city. It was a few hours away from where we lived and, being away with my sister, I knew I now had to adjust. I had to become her advocate, motivator, counselor, and brother. For at least seven days, it was just the two of us in that ICU unit. On some days I felt weak, tired, confused, and even afraid. I knew it was just us in this strange city and having to submit to the care of complete strangers, doctors, and specialists, I got overwhelmed. One particular night, my sister and I were both exhausted. She had been subjected to a lot of tests and pricks and pokes with needles. I was emotionally drained from asking so many questions, trying to be alert and mentally sharp. My brain was spinning as I attempted to remember why they did this or that test. All while monitoring the added risk associated with trying different medications and monitoring her response and hoping and praying for the best.

    As my sister finally fell asleep, I sat in the chair in the corner of that little room and cried. I asked God to heal my sister and give me strength to be what she needed at that moment. As I felt the tears fall, my silent prayer was interrupted by a nurse I had never seen before. I didn't want her to see me crying, so I quickly wiped my face and greeted her. With a warm smile, she politely said, "I'm here to take her vitals." I watched her do what the other nurse had done every hour, however she did something a little different. She leaned over my sister's bed after she had taken her blood pressure and temperature. I heard her say these words I will never forget: *"Young lady, I know you're wondering "why me" right now and none of this is making any sense to you now, but it will later. God has a bigger plan for your life, and you will encourage many people, you're going to be alright."* She then nodded to me and peacefully walked out of the room. I felt an overwhelming sense of peace. I sat back in the chair and drifted off to sleep as well. The next morning, I remembered the words of that nurse and I asked my sister if she heard them. She didn't even remember a nurse coming into the room but told me that night was the first time she slept well since she had the stroke. I realized that the nurse was an angel, and her words gave me hope and strengthened my faith. At that moment, Hebrews 13:2 became alive to me: "...be not forgetful to entertain strangers: for thereby some have entertained angels unaware..." Those words were not only for my sister, but for me as well. That same day, my sister's body began to respond positively to treatments, and they decided to move her back home to start rehabilitation.

Those simple, kind words from that nurse gave me hope and assurance. They caused me to adjust my feelings and adapt my expectations and hopes, just like the willow tree. One of my favorite artists, India Arie, has so many encouraging songs, but in particular a song called, "Break the shell." This song really causes me to think, adapt, and consider personal things I am dealing with. A few words in the song say, "Child it's time to break the shell, life's gonna hurt but it meant to be felt you cannot touch the sky from inside yourself, a bird cannot fly until it breaks the shell...". Life has a way of causing us all to stay in our comfort zones, or shells, but as my grandmother would say, "God has a way that's mighty sweet." God allows life's challenges to cause discomfort and turbulence, but this causes us to adjust, adapt, and thrive, just like the willow tree. When we look back and reflect on how far we have come and where we are now, it will give us fuel for our future. Let's all take a note from one of God's beautiful creations, the willow tree, and remember we were built to bend, adjust, adapt, and thrive. (Psalms 1:3 & 92:12-14)

Day 1 Scriptures

Philippians 4:11-13 (ESV)

11 Not that I am speaking of being in need, for I have learned in whatever situation I am to be content. 12 I know how to be brought low, and I know how to abound. In any and every

Hebrews 13:2 (ESV)

2 Do not neglect to show hospitality to strangers, for thereby some have entertained angels unawares.

Psalms 1:3

He is like a tree planted by streams of water that yields its fruit in its season, and its leaf does not wither. In all that he does, he prospers.

Psalms 92:12-14

The righteous flourish like the palm tree and grow like a cedar in Lebanon.
13 They are planted in the house of the Lord; they flourish in the courts of our God.
14 They still bear fruit in old age; they are ever full of sap and green,

Write it out

Use the bonus journal section to write your day 1 reflections.

Day 2
Essential Needs

Absolute, necessary, and indispensable are just a few words to describe the word essential. The year 2020 will always go down in history as one of the most memorable years ever. It is from this year that our world was turned upside-down because of an invisible virus's deadly effects. This virus not only infected, but it also affected the whole world: we became faced with a new way of living and a new normal. We suddenly found ourselves using words that we normally would not use; words like pandemic, social distancing, social media, mask, virus, and vaccinations. The entire world was shut down, it appeared as if time and days moved slowly, and freedom and mobility had become regulated to standards issued by the government. This experience also made us focus on so many things we took for granted. We see value in minor things; things which have now become what we consider and call essential needs and essential workers. The local grocery store worker, city sanitation workers, and mobile delivery drivers had become key components of our life and our new normal. This global pandemic brought awareness to so many things that we took for granted and now, we ask ourselves what really matters. Even though these things we consider are essential or physical, we cannot neglect the things that are essential to move up and forward emotionally. Here are 5 spiritual essentials that will nurture your mental needs to live a whole and complete life:

1. **Pray without ceasing** (1 Thessalonians 5:17).
   Prayer can shift our mind into alignment with the Creator through communication. Prayer is dialogue, not monologue. After you have a scheduled time of daily prayer, make sure you allow yourself to sit, meditate, and

allow God to speak back to you. He whispers peace, comfort, and direction that only you can hear through prayer and meditation.

2. **Trust in the Lord** (Proverbs 3:5).

Trust is always earned, cultivated, and strengthened through one's experience. When we put our trust in God, it is most likely we will not experience severe disappointment or let-down. Trusting in God always seems to work out to our advantage. It is because of our trust in Him that we have survived the things of our past and can navigate and anticipate greater for the future.

3. **Be alert** (1 Peter 5:8)

Being alert brings awareness, and awareness will always bring change. When we become aware of negative emotions and thought patterns, we can start to do what is necessary to make adjustments for change. We cannot allow life's problems, trials, and negative circumstances to make us emotionally intoxicated with things that are temporary and subject to change. When we are alert, we also make clear, complete, decisions and choices that are best for us and will most likely yield a positive outcome.

4. **Guard your heart** (Proverbs 4:23)

The heart is a strange thing. Physically, it is the only muscle in the body that must beat 100% at all times. The heart is the house of our emotions and the seat of our soul; ironically, the heart and the mind are both connected. When things are conceived in the mind, they take residence in the heart. We must learn to guard and keep our heart and be careful of the things and the people we allow into our heart. Forgiveness is extremely essential for a healthy heart. Learning from past mistakes and navigating through the disappointment of those dear to you are vital for maintaining a healthy spiritual and emotional heart. Oftentimes, we must make the personal decision to choose to heal our hearts from old wounds and move forward in life.

5. **Never lose hope.** (Romans 15:13)

Aspiration, anticipation, belief, confidence, desire, expectation, endurance, and reliance are all characteristics of hope. Hope is the feeling you have when what is wanted can be had, or the belief that events will turn out for the best. Remember that hope and faith are connected. The Bible even tells us in the book of Hebrews (11:1) that faith is the substance of things hoped for and the evidence of things not seen. Hope is the thing that inspires you to get back up and try again when life knocks you down, or when things don't go the way you planned. Hope always causes you to see the light at the end of the tunnel and inspires you to live to see another day. Hope is necessary to obtain victory in every area of your life and allows you to see the light at the end of the tunnel.

Day 2 Scriptures

1 Thessalonians 5:16-18
16 Rejoice always, 17 pray without ceasing, 18 in everything give thanks; for this is the will of God in Christ Jesus for you.

Proverbs 3:5-6
Trust in the Lord with all your heart   and lean not on your own understanding;6 in all your ways submit to him,   and he will make your paths straight.

1st Peter 5:8
Be alert and of sober mind. Your enemy the devil prowls around like a roaring lion looking for someone to devour.

Proverbs 4:23
1 Above all else, guard your heart,   for everything you do flows from it.

Romans 15:13
May the God of hope fill you with all joy and peace as you trust in him, so that you may overflow with hope by the power of the Holy Spirit.

Write it out

Don't forget to journal! Use the bonus journaling section to write your day 2 reflections.

Day 3
You're ABLE

Ableness is so important to mental health and stability. "...And God is able to make all grace abound to you so that always having all sufficiency in everything you may have abundance for every good deed;"(2Corinthians9:8). Mental capacity means being able to make your own decisions; someone lacking that capacity is considered disabled, or as having a mental disability. For 20 years, I worked with the Duval County Public School System as a community-based instructor for students with disabilities. I worked with a wide range of students of many different nationalities, many of whom were identified as lacking mental and/or physical capacity, or wellness. Working in this field increased my knowledge in several ways when it came to people and disabilities. Two of the most intriguing disabilities I've ever worked with are autism and TMH (trainable mentally handicap). Most of those students looked like everybody else and possessed no physical deformities. However, their lack of social skills, emotional levels of communication, and cognitive responses altered how they reacted in simple situations and daily problem-solving tasks. They were either overly or underly social and that negatively influenced and affected how they interacted with the community and society. As their vocational instructor, I had to identify the students' weaknesses and strengths as well as come up with a strategy/plan which allowed them to achieve mental stability; to live a productive life. In other words, it was my assignment to enhance and empower their Ableness. Having unusual or superior intelligence and skill are components of ableness. Mental ableness causes you to be empowered, with a sense of authority over your personal affairs and choices. So, you may also live whole, complete lives and achieve goals, here are a few things to help you remember that you are "ABLE" to handle life and have mentally sound days.

A - Accountability- being accountable to leadership, a mentor, or someone you greatly respect promotes personal discipline and humility. It gives you a sense of responsibility knowing that there are others who have poured into you and believe in you and want to see you reach a desired level of success. (Proverbs 27:17, Heb. 11:17)

B - Balance- find, create, and maintain balance in every area of your life. Give everyone and everything it's proper amount of time, learn to move on and transition at the right time. Take in and hold dear the good experiences and pleasant memories. Release, let go, and learn from every negative encounter. In the words of Dr. Seuss, "Don't cry because it's over, smile because it happened." (Ecclesiastes 7:16)

L - Learning- learning increases our value. It is said the more you know, the more you grow. In life, we never stop learning; make it a habit to learn something new as often as you can. Learning also increases self-esteem and self-worth. By learning something new, you keep the mind and heart relevant in this ever-changing world, while also increasing the sense of knowing. (Proverbs 1:5)

E - Excellence- doing things in excellence will always leave a lasting impression on the people you meet, as well as the people you are connected too. Excellence demands respect. People remember things done in excellence. Steve Martin said it best when he said, "Be so good they can't ignore you." The Bible says that Daniel was known as a man of excellence; this excellence gave him favor with people of influence. Excel is the root word to the word excellent and it means to rise to the highest place, or to obtain an accomplishment or achievement. You cannot be mediocre and excellent at the same time, so choose to do things well and at the highest level of expectation and prepare to experience unlimited satisfaction and mental wholeness. (2 Corinthians 8:7, Daniel 6:3)

Day 3 Scriptures

Proverbs 27:17
As iron sharpens iron, so one person sharpens another.

Hebrews 11:17
17 By faith Abraham, when God tested him, offered Isaac as a sacrifice. He who had embraced the promises was about to sacrifice his one and only son,

Ecclesiastes 7:16
Do not be over-righteous, neither be overwise— why destroy yourself?

Proverbs 1:5
let the wise listen and add to their learning, and let the discerning get guidance—

2 Corinthians 8:7
7 But since you excel in everything—in faith, in speech, in knowledge, in complete earnestness and in the love we have kindled in you[a]—see that you also excel in this grace of giving.

Daniel 6:3
lNow Daniel so distinguished himself among the administrators and the satraps by his exceptional qualities that the king planned to set him over the whole kingdom.

Write it out

Complete your day 3 with a journal reflection.

Day 4
Needful Mindfulness

Most Christians are not familiar with mindfulness and are skeptical because it's associated with other beliefs; however, Christian faith-based counselors use mindfulness in a Christ-integrated way as a therapy tool. Mindfulness is awareness of thoughts and emotions; it includes your feelings, physically and mentally. We often go through our days, weeks, and months without the thought of mindfulness. Mindfulness is often used in meditation and for mental sobriety. Being in ministry and always serving to meet the needs of others has brought me an awareness of the need for mindfulness. The Bible gives us a great concept of mindfulness in Philippians 4:8… "Finally brothers and sisters, whatever is true, whatever is noble, whatever is right, whatever is pure, whatever is lovely, whatever is admirable; if anything is excellent or praiseworthy, think about these things…". Mindfulness gives needful direction for our thoughts. There are days, weeks, even months, where I barely watch any television or listen to radio stations. I enjoy the clarity and soundness of silence; it works for me and keeps me centered. Long drives and barefoot walks on the beach are also helpful. These simple practices increase our ability to regulate emotions and help decrease stress, eliminate anxiety, and conquer depression. When practicing the need for mindfulness, you will notice your focus, attention, and clarity of thoughts will increase. In the Bible, the book of Psalms is one of my favorites because there are Psalms to read for every situation in your life. It also gives a few scripture meditations on mindfulness (Psalms 104: 34, 119:15, & 143:5). David did not write all of the Psalms, but he wrote quite a bit of them; they were birthed out of his experience and testimony about our God. David often had to shift his thinking to succeed as a great leader. I will often find a mindfulness quote or affirmation to read and recite to stimulate positive thoughts and the need for mindfulness. Here are a few that have motivated and encouraged me recently.

Try to love yourself as much as you want someone else to.
(Unknown)

Sometimes the smallest things take up the most room in your heart
(A.A. Milne)

Don't give your past the power to define your future
(Dhiren Prajapati)

Just because you're struggling doesn't mean you are failing.
(Unknown)

H. O. P. E.
Hold On Pain Ends
(unknown)

If you get tired, learn to rest but don't quit.
(Lauren Gleisberg)

Day 4 Scriptures

Philippians 4:8 (KJV)
8 Finally, brethren, whatsoever things are true, whatsoever things are honest, whatsoever things are just, whatsoever things are pure, whatsoever things are lovely, whatsoever things are of good report; if there be any virtue, and if there be any praise, think on these things.

Psalms 104: 34 (KJV)
34 My meditation of him shall be sweet: I will be glad in the Lord.

Psalms 119:15 (NIV)
I meditate on your precepts
and consider your ways.

Psalms 143:5
I remember the days of long ago;
I meditate on all your ways and consider what your hands have done.

Write it out

How can you practice mindfulness in your life today?

Day 5
Transformers

As a young man, I remember growing up watching an animation entitled *Transformers*. The unique thing about the Transformers is they had the ability to transform to what they needed to be when the proper time arose. On the surface, they look like trucks, cars, airplanes...etc, but inside of them was their true identity. They actually were gladiator robots that could shift or transform into warriors who defended their beliefs and protected those they cared about. What I remember most was a phrase in their theme song; *"...Transformers, more than what meets the eye..."*. Spiritually, we can learn a lot from these animated characters. The apostle Paul tells us in the book of Romans that we are not to conform but transform.

Conform means to comply, to become similar in form, nature, or character; transform means to change in condition, nature or character. What makes these two words interesting is that they are both activated or stimulated in the mind. The mind is a powerful thing; it shapes our character, thoughts, and reality. Continuously shifting or renewing our mental state can transform a negative experience into a positive encounter, it can fill a dark day with hope for a brighter tomorrow. Renewing the mind through positive thought, daily prayer, physical activity, and eliminating negative energy (influences), makes us just as interesting as the animated characters I grew up watching.

When the mind is renewed, you become more than what meets the eye; you become a shifter instead of conforming to negative things. You transform, as the scripture says, and move on to prove what is good, acceptable, and perfect. In April of 2017, I received news from my doctor that was negative. It made me feel sad and deeply depressed, however when I connected to those who I know loved and believed in me, they made me transform, and not conform. They began to pour hope and life into me, encouraging me to make better, healthier choices as well as look more toward the future and better days ahead. 2 Corinthians 3:18 & 5:17 are two awesome scriptures that renewed my mind and assisted in transformation. We are indeed transformers, constantly shifting our reality to become what and who God has predestined us to be.

Day 5 Scriptures

Romans 12:2
...and be not conformed to this world but be ye transformed by the renewing of your mind that you may prove what is good and acceptable and perfect will of God...

2 Corinthians 3:18
Trust in the Lord with all your heart and lean not on your own understanding;6 in all your ways submit to him, and he will make your paths straight.

2 Corinthians 5:17
Be alert and of sober mind. Your enemy the devil prowls around like a roaring lion looking for someone to devour.

Write it out
What are your day 5 thoughts?

Day 6
Musical Medication

"Music is truly the universal language, and when it is excellently expressed how deeply it moves our souls."
-David O. Mckay

Never underestimate the power of music or the power of a song. Music plays an intricate part in our everyday living. Music will always connect our mind, memory, and moments. The Bible also shares events when music influenced the moods of others, especially in the life of David who was known as the sweet Psalmist of Israel. One instance involved a song that caused King Saul to develop enmity in his heart against David. After David won a great victory by killing Goliath, the women in the village began to sing a song *"Saul slain thousands but David 10,000"* (1Samuel 18:7). This simple song caused jealousy to grow in the heart of the king toward David. Later in the scriptures, we see that Saul was being tormented by an evil spirit and it was David and his skillfulness in playing an instrument that was the only thing which would soothe the king during those times of tournament. Today, music has that same effect on people and their moods. The Bible says, "for the spirit of heaviness put on a garment of praise" (Isaiah 61:3). The influence of music has a way of molding and transitioning our moods and our mind, especially during times of sadness and sorrow. Have ever received a prescription from your doctor designed to help, but realized the side effects were not worth it? Just as medications have known side-effects, so does music.

There are days and times in my life where I have to monitor my music to motivate my mood. The side effects of music can either be positive or negative. For example, if a person is experiencing a bad break up or even divorce, listening to ballads or love songs is probably not a good idea. When I'm working out in the gym, listening to fast, upbeat music, pushing through an exhausting workout, somehow, I feel like time is moving swiftly. Before I know it, I have whizzed through an hour and a half workout like it was nothing. I have learned to combine prayer with music to modify my mood, refocus my mind, and shift my emotions. Music also helps you communicate when you can't verbally find what to say during prayer. You can say it with a song. I encourage you to find a song that dedicates your day to God and good feelings, especially in the morning as you start your day. Listen to songs that will get you through whatever season that you find yourself in. Music is indeed the soul's mental medication. (Psalms 104:33 & 105:2)

Up & Forward: 30 Day Devotional

Day 6
Scriptures

1 Samuel 18:7 (NIV)
7 As they danced, they sang: "Saul has slain his thousands, and David his tens of thousands."

Isaiah 61:3 (KJV)
3 To appoint unto them that mourn in Zion, to give unto them beauty for ashes, the oil of joy for mourning, the garment of praise for the spirit of heaviness; that they might be called trees of righteousness, the planting of the Lord, that he might be glorified.

Psalms 104:33
33 I will sing unto the Lord as long as I live: I will sing praise to my God while I have my being.

Psalms 105:2
2 Sing unto him, sing psalms unto him: talk ye of all his wondrous works.

Write it out

What songs assist in modifying your mood and refocusing your mind ?

EMOTIONALLY

A life without emotions is a bland life indeed, for it is our emotions which influence our feelings. To be overcome with emotions is a common, natural thing, but learning how to manage them takes discipline and practice. When someone does something kind or nice to you, it makes you feel happy. When you lose a relative or experience death, it makes you feel sad. We must remember that we were created in the image of God and God has emotions and feelings. God is the God of love and joy. Happiness flows from Him. God also feels anger, especially to those who constantly disobey His commands. God also releases compassion and mercy to those who embraced Him. The Bible lets us know that Jesus himself dealt with a wide range of emotions. Scripture tells us, "He was a man of sorrow acquainted with grief." We even see in the Bible that he wept during the death of his friend, Lazarus. He also got angry for the misuse of his father's house. God created us with a wide range of emotional capabilities. We can express as He does and be disciplined enough to keep our emotions under control. It is our governing and control of our emotions that can cause us to live fruitful, balanced lives. There are several examples in the Bible of people who were emotionally overwhelmed. Let's take Joseph, for example (Gen.43:30) He was mistreated by his brothers, thrown into a pit, sold into slavery, sent to prison, then later elevated into leadership in Egypt. Seeing his brothers years later, not knowing who he was, they asked for help in the midst of a famine. Joseph recognized that these were his brothers, but they did not recognize him. He became emotionally overwhelmed; the Bible says he hurried from the room because he was overcome with emotion. He went into a private room, broke down, and wept.

Joseph did not suppress his emotions, but he did keep them in check and under control. We are never to suppress or ignore our emotions; we have to learn to govern, manage, and control them. Anger, fear, disgust, happiness, sadness, surprise, and contempt are the most common emotions that we experience daily. At times, our emotions may feel unmanageable, but they are not; we actually have a choice. We must choose to manage our emotions. Mismanaged emotions can have a real negative affect on our physical well-being. Stressing and worrying can lead to ulcers, high blood pressure, sleepless nights, weight problems, headaches, and many other negative effects on the body. We take control of our emotions when we control our response. Daily prayer, reading the word of God, and submitting to the Holy Spirit will certainly help manage emotions. This will assist in controlling our response to life's situations to live an emotionally sound, and balanced life.

Day 7
Feelings are Not Facts
"For as a man thinks in his heart so is he" (Prov 23:7)

It's so amazing to know the heart and the mind are both connected. The Bible says in Proverbs, as a man thinks in his heart, so is he, the things we think somehow have a way of resting, germinating, and growing in the heart. The heart is a strange thing: physically, it is the only muscle in the body that must beat at 100% every time. Emotionally, the heart is the birthplace of our feelings, which influences our emotions. (Proverbs 4:23)

How many times have you ever made the statement *"I'm going to follow my heart"* and that ended up being one of the worst decisions you have ever made? Most of the time when we follow our heart, we are actually following our feelings, and when we are guided by our feelings, our feelings become our facts. That can lead us down a long road of disappointment. We must take note and remember that our emotions come from thoughts, attitudes, opinions, desires, and beliefs; these things are all governed and come from the heart. Jeremiah 17:9, "says the heart is deceitful above all things and desperately wicked who can know it." I personally had to learn to take my heart out of some decisions because my heart was causing me to make decisions based on how I felt. I realized my feelings were not facts and were often unreliable. Feelings can have you painting a scenario and picture of a situation that's not even true.

When we take just a few minutes to pray and think before we react or respond to any situation, most of the time, our outcome and response will be more positive and productive. Taking the time to sit and think before we respond gives us time to evaluate the situation and sort out our emotions. In those moments of thinking, you exercise self-control and will more likely give a wiser response. James chapter 1 verse 19 is truly something to consider and exercise daily so our emotions won't cause us to make the wrong decision based on how we feel. Think before you speak, pray before you do, and check the facts before you submit to any feeling!

Day 7 Scriptures

Proverbs 23:7 (KJV)
7 For as he thinketh in his heart, so is he

Proverbs 4:23 (NIV)
Above all else, guard your heart,
for everything you do flows from it.

Jeremiah 17:9 (NIV)
9 The heart is deceitful above all things, and
desperately wicked: who can know it?

James 1:19 (KJV)
19 My dear brothers and sisters, take note of this:
Everyone should be quick to listen, slow to speak
and slow to become angry,

Write it out

What emotions are you wrestling with today?

Day 8
Emotional Enemy

> *"... then he said take the arrows so he took them and he said to the king of Israel strike the ground so he struck three times and stopped and the man of God was angry with him and said you should have struck five or six times then you would have struck Syria till you had destroyed it but now you'll straight Syria only three times.." (2Kings 13:18-19)*

Second Kings chapter 13 gives us an amazing story with a somewhat sad ending that did not have to end in such a way. In this particular chapter, you see the King Joash who heavily relied on the prophet Elijah. It is very clear that he had a deep personal relationship with Elijah, he even referred to him as his father. At this moment in the scripture, Elijah was on his deathbed and the king goes to visit him and get instructions for one last time. As Elijah gives the kings instructions that will give him promised victory throughout his reign, the king allows his emotions to get in the way. These emotions cause him to turn what could have been a season of unlimited victory into only 3 years, then defeat thereafter.

This biblical story is all too common to so many of us. We have often missed out on some of the greatest seasons of our lives because of an emotional response. This story also reveals to us how we can experience emotional disappointment depending solely on others and not depending on God. This happens when we make people our everything and give them seats and thrones in our hearts that are higher than God. If we lose them or the relationship becomes strained, we feel as if we have no hope. Our days seem dark, while our disappointed feelings cause us to sink into anger, sadness, and depression. We can often become our own enemies when we allow our own uncontrolled emotions to lead our decisions and choices. "...A man without self-control is like a city with broken- down walls." Prov 25:28. We all must understand that emotions impact judgment. When you are feeling overwhelmed and disappointment has gripped your heart, remember to stop, identify, and deactivate the negative trigger points. Say a prayer, then take a moment to think and evaluate what has happened. Take note that a wise response is better than a negative reaction. Psalm 19:14

# Day 8 Scriptures

2 Kings 13:18-19

.. then he said take the arrows so he took them and he said to the king of Israel strike the ground so he struck three times and stopped and the man of God was angry with him and said you should have struck five or six times then you would have struck Syria till you had destroyed it but now you'll straight Syria only three times..

Proverbs 25:28

Trust in the Lord with all your heart and lean not on your own understanding;6 in all your ways submit to him, and he will make your paths straight.

Pslam 19:14

Be alert and of sober mind. Your enemy the devil prowls around like a roaring lion looking for someone to devour.

Don't forget to write your day 8 reflections!

Day 9
Altered Anger

Anger is often the one emotion that gets a bad reputation. However, anger is one of the most important emotions God has empowered us to have. Yes, God is a God of love but he's also a God of anger (Exodus 15:7). Throughout the Bible, you will often read of God's anger being kindled. Anger often reveals a person's boundaries and their values. Once those things have been violated, anger is usually the emotion which is displayed. Anger can often reveal a lot about oneself. Anger usually happens after awareness has occurred and the display of anger is often the response. Jesus got angry when he saw the misuse of his father's house (Matt 21:12-17). This display of anger showed us that Jesus had a strong passion toward the things of his father (the Kingdom of God). We all defend what we love, especially when we feel it has been endangered or threatened. Ephesians 4:26-27 "be angry and sin not let not the sun go down upon your wrath: neither give place to the devil…". When anger is not dealt with or confronted, the enemy uses imagination and assumption to paint a false scenario to make things seem worse than they actually are.

Anger is most productive when it is not suppressed, but emotionally altered. Altered anger is simply anger that is rationalized and thought out, instead of responding quickly and irrationally. Altered anger is a response that has been emotionally processed and handled with prayer. It's always good to have a listening ear or someone to confide in to discuss the situation that has made you angry. This makes you open to other perspectives. Proverbs 11:14 helps us understand the benefits of a listening ear and wise counsel. When you realize anger *(when displayed*) has impact, you become aware of its power and influence. You then monitor or alter your response for a more favorable outcome or resolve. Anger that's not in control can be dangerous. We must realize not all anger is bad; anger must be dealt with, confronted, and never suppressed, especially when it's motive is geared toward the defense of the things of God, righteousness, justice, and the disadvantage of others. Oftentimes it takes anger to bring about change. Moses would've never brought Israel out of Egypt if he had not gotten angry witnessing the mistreatment of a Hebrew slave; he reacted out of anger and it brought about a change. Dr. Martin Luther King Jr. and several other civil rights activists would have never made positive strides if they did not wisely deal with the anger of injustice that they, and several other minorities, received. These great leaders altered their response during angry situations and brought about significant change. When anger is motivated by finding a solution, rather than actionless venting it can prove to be most productive to oneself and others. (Psalms 37:8), (Proverbs 14:29)

Day 9 Scriptures

Exodus 15:7
And in the greatness of Your excellence
You have overthrown those who rose against You;
You sent forth Your wrath;
It consumed them like stubble.

Ephesians 4:26-27
26 Be ye angry, and sin not: let not the sun go down upon your wrath: 27 Neither give place to the devil.

Proverbs 11:14
14 Where no counsel is, the people fall: but in the multitude of counsellors there is safety

Psalms 37:8
8 Cease from anger, and forsake wrath: fret not thyself in any wise to do evil.

Proverbs 14:29
29 He that is slow to wrath is of great understanding: but he that is hasty of spirit exalteth folly.

Write it out

How can you respond to anger in a healthy way today?

Day 10
Fruit Filled

"Buy this my father is glorified, that you may bear much fruit so you will be my disciples" (John 15:8)

As disciples and followers of Christ, we have been commissioned to live a fruit filled life. Most people focus on being fruitful until they miss the commission that we have to be fruit filled. We must become fruit producers. Fruitfulness pushes and compels us to strive to be productive and successful concerning the things around us. It influences our ambitions, our goals, and our motives. All of those are good, but we must remember: we must also produce things that exemplify Christ and his teachings. The word disciple simply means, "a follower or student of..." so if we are truly Christ's disciples, then fruit bearing should be our common nature and characteristic. Galatians 5:22-23 tells us the fruit that Christ's disciples should display: love, joy, peace, long-suffering, kindness, goodness, faithfulness, gentleness, self-control, and all spiritual fruits that are rooted in our emotions. Through daily prayer, the study of God's word, and a personal connection with God, these fruits become seedlings and germinate in our heart and mind. Once they are produced in our everyday life, we can then enjoy a true sense of fulfillment. spiritually and physically. God gets the glory out of our lives when these fruits are displayed. "No good tree bears bad fruit, nor does a bad tree bear good fruit. Each tree is recognized by its own fruit. People do not pick figs from the thorn bushes or grapes from briars. A good man brings good things out of the good stored up in his heart, and an evil man brings evil things out of the evil stored up in his heart.." (Luke 6:43-45). We have all been called to produce. We produce after our likeness and kind. It is the heart that germinates the seeds of our character fruits. You will produce what's in your heart. When the heart is good, the fruit is good. God smiles on us and causes us to flourish and live a fruit filled life. (Psalm 92:12-15)

Day 10 Scriptures

Galatians 5:22-23

22 But the fruit of the Spirit is love, joy, peace, longsuffering, gentleness, goodness, faith,23 Meekness, temperance: against such there is no law.

Proverbs 25:28

Trust in the Lord with all your heart   and lean not on your own understanding;6 in all your ways submit to him,   and he will make your paths straight.

Luke 6:43-45

43 For a good tree bringeth not forth corrupt fruit; neither doth a corrupt tree bring forth good fruit.44 For every tree is known by his own fruit. For of thorns men do not gather figs, nor of a bramble bush gather they grapes.45 A good man out of the good treasure of his heart bringeth forth that which is good; and an evil man out of the evil treasure of his heart bringeth forth that which is evil: for of the abundance of the heart his mouth speaketh.

Psalm 92:12-15

12 The righteous shall flourish like the palm tree: he shall grow like a cedar in Lebanon.13 Those that be planted in the house of the Lord shall flourish in the courts of our God.14 They shall still bring forth fruit in old age; they shall be fat and flourishing;15 To shew that the Lord is upright: he is my rock, and there is no unrighteousness in him.

Don't forget to write your day 10 reflections!

Day 11
Almost

A few words that describe "almost" include not quite, all but, close to, very nearly, and just about. The power of the word almost is quite often overlooked. Almost, when seen and used in an optimistic point of view, can positively work for you and shift your emotions toward a favorable outcome. Asaph wrote in Psalm 73:2, "but as for me my feet had almost stumbled; my steps had nearly slipped…" Psalms is one of my favorite Bible books to read because there is a Psalm written for every situation in your life; they are like spiritual antibiotics. Psalm 73 shows how the writer almost gave up when he observed and envied the prosperity of the wicked. We, like Asaph, have compared ourselves to others which can often lead to a road of despair and even depression. However, I love how in verse 17 & 26 of Psalms 73. Asaphs experience and relationship with God to remind him of the fate of the wicked. He gathered his emotions together and began to give God glory, knowing that at any moment, things are subject to turn in his favor. When we can all view "almost" in another light, it will send us into personal a praise. When you consider all the negative things that almost happened but didn't; when you consider the days you almost felt like giving up, but you pushed forward and made it through. When you take note and see the victory in those things that did not happen, and how that somehow worked out for your good, then you can see the value of almost. I'm so glad Almost doesn't count. (Psalms 119:87)

 **Day 11 Scriptures**

Psalm 73:2
but as for me my feet had almost stumbled; my steps had nearly slipped...

Psalm 73: 17
17 till I entered the sanctuary of God; then I understood their final destiny..

Psalm 73:26
My flesh and my heart may fail, but God is the strength of my heart and my portion forever.

Psalms 119:85-88
86 All your commands are trustworthy; help me, for I am being persecuted without cause.
87 They almost wiped me from the earth, but I have not forsaken your precepts.
88 In your unfailing love preserve my life, that I may obey the statutes of your mouth.

Write it out

Complete the sentence in the journaling section for day 11...
"I almost..but I am so glad God..."

Day 12
Just do it

What do you do when God's answer does not look like your request? We can learn a lot from a man named Naman (2 Kings chapter 5). The Bible says Naaman was a man of war; well-respected and greatly admired by many, but he had an issue: he was a leper. Naaman's issue was hidden; very few people knew about it, only his wife and a few of his close servants. It was his beloved servant girl, who admired him greatly, who suggested to Naaman's wife that he should go see the prophet Elisha so he could be healed. When the king became aware of Naaman's issues, and that there was someone who could heal, the king valued him so much and invested in his healing. He sent Naaman to see the prophet with money and other valuable gifts. It's always interesting to know that God will send people into your life who will invest in your better. Once Naaman got into the presence of the prophet, his expectations were challenged, and he almost missed his miracle and healing. Naamans emotional reaction almost caused him to noy get the very thing he came seeking after, only because the method the prophet gave him was not what he expected. He expected the prophet to come lay hands on him, or do something mythical, but the prophet told him to go dip in dirty water to become clean. He almost went back home, but his beloved servant said something to him that allowed him to get his emotions in check. The servant said to him simply, just do it, he did not ask a hard thing, just do it. Because of Naamans obedience, although he was reluctant, he did it; and he was completely healed. Life is filled with risk and gambles, but I have found that when we meet God in prayer, often, His instructions will not look like our expectations.

However, we must do the same thing that the servant told Naaman; just do it. We will not always have the details, so stop wrestling with the how, the when, the why, and the where; just do it and watch how God allows you to reach your goals and supersede every expectation. (Isaiah 55:8)

Day 12 Scriptures

2nd Kings 5-6

Now Naaman was commander of the army of the king of Aram. He was a great man in the sight of his master and highly regarded, because through him the Lord had given victory to Aram. He was a valiant soldier, but he had leprosy.[a] 2 Now bands of raiders from Aram had gone out and had taken captive a young girl from Israel, and she served Naaman's wife. 3 She said to her mistress, "If only my master would see the prophet who is in Samaria! He would cure him of his leprosy." 4 Naaman went to his master and told him what the girl from Israel had said. 5 "By all means, go," the king of Aram replied. "I will send a letter to the king of Israel." So Naaman left, taking with him ten talents[b] of silver, six thousand shekels[c] of gold and ten sets of clothing. 6 The letter that he took to the king of Israel read: "With this letter I am sending my servant Naaman to you so that you may cure him of his leprosy."

Isaiah 55:8

"For my thoughts are not your thoughts,
neither are your ways my ways,"
declares the Lord.

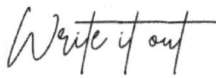

Use the journal prompt below to complete your day 12 reflection.
"Today I am committed to doing...:

SPIRITUALLY

Let me start by saying, spirituality is not mythical or spooky. To be spiritual has nothing to do with religion or denomination. Spirituality, in simple form, is connecting one's spirit to God's spirit. We must remember that there is absolutely nothing human or fleshly about God, He is spirit. (John 4:24.. "God is Spirit…"). When God the creator created us, He created our lives in a symbolic form of the Godhead, the Trinity; God the father, God the son, God the Holy Spirit. We are made in a tricodomic way with spirit, soul, and body. Our spirit is what came from God the Creator, our soul is the residing place of our character and emotions, our body is the earthly dwelling place of which the spirit and soul lives. It is our job to bring all three together in divine balance and harmony. Spirituality with The Creator is cultivated through relationship; the essence of relationship is built by communication. Prayer and meditation bring awareness to spirituality. Because God is a spirit, He is not limited by physical location, He is omnipresent. Genesis chapter 2:7 gives us great insight on how God the Creator created mankind different from other creatures. When he breathed his breath into man's nostrils, it was the breath of life; man became a living creature. His spirit lives in all of us and gives us life. We were created to commune and connect with God, the father and our Creator. There will always be a longing or a yearning in our life to be spiritually connected with something; as we mature and grow in life, so does our consciousness. This consciousness brings awareness of thoughts, feelings, and experiences, and leads us to enlightenment. Personal spirituality brings truth, harmony, balance, and peace to our lives. Romans 8:6 lets us know, to set the mind on the spirit is life. When you are spiritually connected to God, you go beyond existing to truly living. To learn, to experience, to love, to create, is truly living. Truth and freedom are the results of living a life connected spiritually with God the Creator. (John 6:63 ESV), " it is the Spirit who gives life the flesh is no help at all…".

Day 13
The Struggle Is Real

Knowing and living your personal truth is a major part of spirituality. We often go through life living for and pleasing others. We often lose track of who we really are. It becomes a major struggle trying to please everyone and yet have time for self-love and self-care. The Bible tells an amazing story about Jacob, who lived his life in an identity crisis. Jacob had an older twin brother by the name of Esau. The Bible says that even in their mothers' womb, the two brothers struggled. The struggle was so intense that their mother, Rebekah, asked God in prayer what was going on inside of her. The Lord responded saying, "two nations are in your womb two people shall be separated from your body; one will be stronger than the other and the older shall serve the younger." Gen 25:23-26).

Esau grew to be a hunter and more favored by his father, Jacob was more of a homebody and was more favored by his mother. Seeing that their father Isaac was growing older in age, his sight became very dim and it was soon time for the blessing to be passed to the older son. Rebecca and their mother came up with a plan so Jacob could receive the blessing instead of his older twin brother, Esau. Jacob did not want to displease his mother and although he felt uneasy about the plan, he went through with it. Disguised as his brother, he received the blessing from his father, which could not be taken back or reversed. When Esau became aware of what happened, he hated his brother and after the death of his father, he vowed to kill Jacob. Jacob ran for his life. While running from his brother one particular night, he found himself alone, and in being alone, he wrestled with an angel till daybreak.

The interesting thing about this struggle is it happened when everybody was gone from him and he had to deal with it himself. The angel asked a significant question, "What is your name?"; in other words who are you? Jacob struggled, like so many of us, with his identity and wanting the blessings of a father, and not wanting to disappoint his mother. Jacob, being obedient to his mothers scheme of taking on his brothers' identity, blessing, and birthright, was now a fugitive running for his life. Realizing that his brother was catching up to him and would soon meet up with him, to preserve his family, he sent them away ahead of him, and was left alone. As the night approached, he was physically and mentally exhausted. He laid down to rest and saw an open vision of heaven with angels ascending and descending. Suddenly, he was alarmed by a force with the appearance of a man. They begin to wrestle and as they wrestled, Jacob was asked an important question, *"What is your name?"* For the first time in Jacob's life, he gave his true identity. Like Jacob, when we are alone, we are forced to deal with the personal struggle of who we are and the things we have done. When Jacob realized that the person he was wrestling/struggling with was not a natural being, he held on and made a declaration *"I will not let go until you bless me."* There are so many details to the story, but the one that hits me the most is Jacob's determination not to give up or let go even in a struggle.

We all have different struggles in different areas of our lives, especially when it comes to dealing with who we really are, living up to the expectations of others, and giving account to the deeds we have done. When we are determined to hold on until we are blessed, that's when things will begin to change for our life. The struggle is real, but we have the power to overcome it, if only we can just hang in there till day breaks. Daybreak symbolizes change and a new beginning. Job understood it very well when he said, *"all the days of my appointed time I will wait till my change comes"*.(Job 14:14)

Day 13
Scriptures

Genesis 25:23-26

23 And the Lord said unto her, Two nations are in thy womb, and two manner of people shall be separated from thy bowels; and the one people shall be stronger than the other people; and the elder shall serve the younger.24 And when her days to be delivered were fulfilled, behold, there were twins in her womb.25 And the first came out red, all over like an hairy garment; and they called his name Esau.26 And after that came his brother out, and his hand took hold on Esau's heel; and his name was called Jacob: and Isaac was threescore years old when she bare them.

Job 14:14

If someone dies, will they live again?
All the days of my hard service
I will wait for my renewal[a] to come.

Write it out

Don't forget to write your day 13 reflections in the bonus journal section.

Day 14
Command, Control, Create

Jesus was known in many different ways. In Nazareth, he was known as the son of Joseph and Mary. In Heaven, he was known as Emmanuel, the Prince of Peace and the Son of God. In many surrounding towns and villages, he was known as the great prophet, the miracle worker, and some even called him hosanna. To a group of men that sat at his feet and became his disciples, he was known as their teacher, their rabbi. Jesus knew his assignment on earth would be quick, yet impactful. Jesus spent most of his days instructing and teaching the disciples about kingdom living, on earth as it is in heaven. A lot of Jesus' teachings were done through illustrations such as parables, however a great majority of his teachings were on-the-job training and hands-on experiences. The Gospels are very unique because they give the same experiences, but different points of view. In the gospels, many disciples tell the same story, but in a different way. One of those familiar stories are found in the gospels of Matthew (8:23-27, Mark (4:35) and Luke (8:22-25). This experience reveals how Jesus was God and man, both human and divine. Prior to this experience, Jesus had been teaching and ministering all day. He had become fatigued and tired in his body and, like the rest of us, he needed rest. He got on the boat with his disciples and quickly fell asleep. While he was sleeping, there arose a great storm. The storm was so intense that the disciples became nervous and uneasy. In panic, they woke Jesus up. According to Matthew and Luke's gospel they said, "Lord save us we are perishing." Mark's gospel says they said to him, "teacher, do you not care that we are perishing." Both accounts let us know that the storm was extremely intense and it evoked fear in the disciples, but Jesus was so tired, he was sleeping through it. Like the disciples and like Jesus, we will have to experience life's extremes. What helps us through life's extremes is to remember that the Savior is on the ship with us. All we have to do is wake him up. We can wake him up through prayer and praise. Allow him to become active, alive, and awake in every area of your life. Once Jesus was awakened, he taught the disciples a lesson on spiritual authority. He took command when he rebuked the winds; he took control when he spoke to the sea and told it to be still; he created what he wanted to see and the result was a great calmness. Since the Savior now lives in us through the power of the Holy Spirit, we have the ability to take command of every storm-like situation in our lives, control our emotions and reactions, and create the environment we want to see. (Matthew 18:18, Job 22:28)

Day 14 Scriptures

Matthew 8:23-27

23 And when he was entered into a ship, his disciples followed him.24 And, behold, there arose a great tempest in the sea, insomuch that the ship was covered with the waves: but he was asleep.25 And his disciples came to him, and awoke him, saying, Lord, save us: we perish.26 And he saith unto them, Why are ye fearful, O ye of little faith? Then he arose, and rebuked the winds and the sea; and there was a great calm.27 But the men marvelled, saying, What manner of man is this, that even the winds and the sea obey him!

Ephesians 4:26-27

35 And the same day, when the even was come, he saith unto them, Let us pass over unto the other side.

Luke 8:22-25)

14 Where no counsel is, the people fall: but in the multitude of counsellors there is safety

Matthew 18:18

18 Verily I say unto you, Whatsoever ye shall bind on earth shall be bound in heaven: and whatsoever ye shall loose on earth shall be loosed in heaven.

Job 22:28

28 Thou shalt also decree a thing, and it shall be established unto thee: and the light shall shine upon thy ways.

Write it out

Write your day 14 reflections in the journal section.

Day 15
The Odds are in Your Favor

Odds are the chances or the likelihood of something happening. Odds reflect probability and ratio; they declare that something is so, or will occur. When the odds are in your favor, you have the edge, the lead, and the advantage. As spirit led believers, cultivated through a personal relationship with God by prayer and studying the Holy scriptures, somehow when the odds are stacked against us, things always seem to fall in our favor. The unexplainable becomes our testimony. "...we overcome by the blood of the lamb and the word of our testimony." The book of Judges is one of the Bible's most interesting books. Judges' main focus is on the people of Israel after the death of Moses and Joshua. Israel did not have a direct leader and they constantly went through cycles of sin, suffering, and salvation. They would fall into sin, God would allow an enemy to overtake them and cause great suffering, they would repent and for salvation, God would raise up a leader among them. Notable leaders include Ehud, Shamgar, Sampson, Deborah, and Gideon (just to name a few). Sampson is one of the most talked about judges, however Gideon is one of the most interesting judges. God called Gideon a mighty man of valor even though he was just the opposite; he was shy, timid, and quite fearful. God did to Gideon what he does to so many of us; he pulled out of Gideon what had been inside of him all along. Paul told us in the book of Romans 4:17…"he who quicken the dead, call of those things which are not as though they were."

To spiritually understand God is to accept that he will sometimes not make any natural sense, but our trust in him will always work for our good and our favor; "...trust in the lord with

Day 15
The Odds are in Your Favor

Odds are the chances or the likelihood of something happening. Odds reflect probability and ratio; they declare that something is so, or will occur. When the odds are in your favor, you have the edge, the lead, and the advantage. As spirit led believers, cultivated through a personal relationship with God by prayer and studying the Holy scriptures, somehow when the odds are stacked against us, things always seem to fall in our favor. The unexplainable becomes our testimony. "...we overcome by the blood of the lamb and the word of our testimony." The book of Judges is one of the Bible's most interesting books. Judges' main focus is on the people of Israel after the death of Moses and Joshua. Israel did not have a direct leader and they constantly went through cycles of sin, suffering, and salvation. They would fall into sin, God would allow an enemy to overtake them and cause great suffering, they would repent and for salvation, God would raise up a leader among them. Notable leaders include Ehud, Shamgar, Sampson, Deborah, and Gideon (just to name a few). Sampson is one of the most talked about judges, however Gideon is one of the most interesting judges. God called Gideon a mighty man of valor even though he was just the opposite; he was shy, timid, and quite fearful. God did to Gideon what he does to so many of us; he pulled out of Gideon what had been inside of him all along. Paul told us in the book of Romans 4:17..."he who quicken the dead, call of those things which are not as though they were."

To spiritually understand God is to accept that he will sometimes not make any natural sense, but our trust in him will always work for our good and our favor; "...trust in the lord with

# Day 14 Scriptures

Matthew 8:23-27
23 And when he was entered into a ship, his disciples followed him.24 And, behold, there arose a great tempest in the sea, insomuch that the ship was covered with the waves: but he was asleep.25 And his disciples came to him, and awoke him, saying, Lord, save us: we perish.26 And he saith unto them, Why are ye fearful, O ye of little faith? Then he arose, and rebuked the winds and the sea; and there was a great calm.27 But the men marvelled, saying, What manner of man is this, that even the winds and the sea obey him!

Ephesians 4:26-27
35 And the same day, when the even was come, he saith unto them, Let us pass over unto the other side.

Luke 8:22-25)
14 Where no counsel is, the people fall: but in the multitude of counsellors there is safety

Matthew 18:18
18 Verily I say unto you, Whatsoever ye shall bind on earth shall be bound in heaven: and whatsoever ye shall loose on earth shall be loosed in heaven.

Job 22:28
28 Thou shalt also decree a thing, and it shall be established unto thee: and the light shall shine upon thy ways.

Write it out

Write your day 14 reflections in the journal section.

all your heart and lean not to your own understanding but acknowledge him in all your ways..."(Proverbs 3:5). God downsized Gideon's army from 32,000 to 10,000, then to 300. God did this so when Gideon and his small army got the victory for Israel, they could only give the glory to God. The Midianites troops numbered about 135,000, to Israel's 300. With God, impossibilities become possibilities; a disadvantage becomes an advantage. The odds appeared to be against them; they were just right for God. The Lord gave Gideon a strategy and a plan that evoked fear and panic in his enemy. Gideon won the victory in the name of the Lord and became known as the mighty man of valor God said he was. This story gives us hope and encourages us to know that when the odds are stacked against us and we can't make any sense out of what's going on, trust and know that the situation is just right for God. Seek God's direction through prayer and allow him to give you a strategy that may not make any sense at the time, but will in the end, lead you to an unexplainable victory. (Zechariah 4:6, psalms 20:7)

 **Day 15 Scriptures**

Romans 4:17
17 (As it is written, I have made thee a father of many nations,) before him whom he believed, even God, who quickeneth the dead, and calleth those things which be not as though they were.

Proverbs 3:5
5 Trust in the Lord with all thine heart; and lean not unto thine own understanding.

Zechariah 4:6
6 Then he answered and spake unto me, saying, This is the word of the Lord unto Zerubbabel, saying, Not by might, nor by power, but by my spirit, saith the Lord of hosts.

Psalms 20:7
7 Some trust in chariots, and some in horses: but we will remember the name of the Lord our God.

Write it out

What are you seeking God's direction for?

Day 16
An Unbelievable Answer

Never underestimate the power of prayer! I remember being a young boy growing up in a praying family: at any moment, my family would start a prayer meeting in my grandmother's house. It did not matter where we were as children; whether in the house watching TV or outside playing, when we heard my grandmother and my aunts inside having prayer, we would stop what we were doing and join the prayer service. Oftentimes, the homes of other neighbors and friends would turn into a pop-up prayer service and I would be right in the midst of them as well. It was from these experiences I witnessed the miracle working power of prayer. I saw many signs and wonders. I did not know what to call it when I was younger, I just knew that after the saints prayed, things got better. Now I know that prayer and faith produces God's power, manifestation, and answers. The Bible gives us an example of a house prayer meeting which produced an unbelievable answer. The book of Acts reveals the birth of the church after the day of Pentecost.

The early church was known for its signs, wonders, and miracles; the things that drew people to the early church. The early church also suffered major persecution and great suffering. In the book of Acts chapter 12:1-16, we read an extraordinary story about the power of prayer and how swiftly God will answer us. At the beginning of this chapter you see how Herod the King stretched out his hand and severely harassed the church. He had James, the brother of John, killed, and when he saw it moved and pleased the crowd of a certain group of people, he seized Peter, arrested him, and planned his crucifixion next. When the early believers heard of this, they gathered at the home of a lady named

Mary to intercede on Peter's behalf and pray for his release. While they were praying, God was already working. The Lord sent an angel to release Peter. God was moving so swiftly that even Peter had to gather himself together. " *...and when Peter had come to himself he said now I know for certain that the Lord has sent his angel and has delivered me...".(verse 11).* Peter gathered himself together and made his way to the house of Mary where a prayer meeting on his behalf was happening. He knocked on the door. A servant girl named Rhoda went to answer the door, heard Peter's voice, and got very excited because the very person they were praying for in the house was now standing outside the house. She ran to tell them that Peter was at the door. They thought she was out of her mind or crazy because they were praying so hard and didn't want to believe her. Peter kept knocking. They eventually answered the door, and the Bible says they were amazed and astonished. Just like this amazing biblical experience, we must understand that the power of prayer is unlimited, and God will often answer our prayers so swiftly it's unbelievable. (Matt 7:7,21:22, Mark 11:24)

Day 16 Scriptures

Matthew 7:7
7 Ask, and it shall be given you; seek, and ye shall find; knock, and it shall be opened unto you:

Matthew 21:22
22 And all things, whatsoever ye shall ask in prayer, believing, ye shall receive.

Mark 11:24
24 Therefore I say unto you, What things soever ye desire, when ye pray, believe that ye receive them, and ye shall have them.

Write it out

What are you praying for today?

Day 17
It's not what it looks like

Being spiritually connected has a lot to do with seeing things from another perspective. Spending consistent time with God will always lead to greater insight because you become familiar with hearing God's voice. Every good relationship has good communication, which often results in clarity and understanding. Greater insight is the direct result of a good relationship. Insight is seeing the true nature of someone or something with a clear, deep understanding and perception of the subject or situation. With insight, you stand firmly on the revelation of what you know. What you know brings stability and you're less likely to be moved by the physical and tangible things that may appear but are not proven.

A gemologist knows the difference between a cubic zirconia and a real diamond just by looking at it. The average person may not know the difference and can easily be fooled, but because the gemologist knows the makeup characteristic and nature of a diamond, they know what to look for and can identify real from fake. This is the kind of insight we gain from consistent prayer and meditation with God. Instead of seeing things in the negative and as a threat, you will be able to look beyond the negative and find the positive. You will truly understand (2Corinthians 5:7) "..for we walk by faith and not by sight". Often, God has to do for us what he did for Elisha's servant in 2Kings 6:15-17. The Syrian army was against Israel, but every time they were going to fight Israel, God would give Israel insight on where their enemies were coming from. The King of Syria inquired, thinking maybe he had a spy in the camp. Later, they informed him that Israel had a seer, a prophet named Elisha who would reveal to them where the enemies were coming from. The King of Syria decided to surround Elijah's house. When Elisha's servant opened the door, he saw an army surrounding the house but he noticed Elisha wasn't panicking, he was not afraid, and he was not upset. God had given him insight, and that insight gave him assurance and peace. Elijah prayed that the Lord would open his servants eyes. When the servant looked again, he saw the Lord's Army with chariots of fire surrounding the house of Elijah and said "there are more for us than those that are against us." God will often give us an eye-opening experience just like Elijah's servant. Something will happen so we can have better insight, clarity, and revelation about the situations we find ourselves in and the God we serve. (Prov 20:12, Hebrews 11:1)

 **Day 17 Scriptures**

2 Corinthians 5:7
7 (For we walk by faith, not by sight:)

Kings 6:15-17
15 And when the servant of the man of God was risen early, and gone forth, behold, an host compassed the city both with horses and chariots. And his servant said unto him, Alas, my master! how shall we do? 16 And he answered, Fear not: for they that be with us are more than they that be with them. 17 And Elisha prayed, and said, Lord, I pray thee, open his eyes, that he may see. And the Lord opened the eyes of the young man; and he saw: and, behold, the mountain was full of horses and chariots of fire round about Elisha.

Proverbs 20:12
12 The hearing ear, and the seeing eye, the Lord hath made even both of them.

Hebrews 11:1
11 Now faith is the substance of things hoped for, the evidence of things not seen.

Write it out

Don't forget to write your day 17 reflections!

Day 18
Storm 101

Isn't it interesting how God often uses storms to teach us life lessons? Most of the time when storms are mentioned in the Bible, there's a lesson to be learned. Life's storms have a way of bringing out the best in you, while revealing the qualities within you. Living in Florida with tropical climates, you become very familiar with storms. When you hear a severe storm is approaching, instead of panicking, you prepare. It's the same situation when it comes to spiritual storms. A consistent life of prayer and praise will prepare, preserve, and teach you how to weather the storm. Matthew 7:24-27 gives us some storm advice, "Everyone who hears these words of mine and does them will be like a wise man who built his house on the rock and the rain fail and the floods came and the wind blew and beat on the house, but it did not fall, because it had been found it on the rock, and everyone who hears these words of mine and does not do them will be like the foolish man who built his house on the sand and the rain fell, and the floods came, and the wind blew and beat against that house, and it fell, and great was the fall of it....". Being rooted and grounded in God through a personal relationship will give you the necessary tools to weather any storm that comes in your life. Naturally there are different types of storms: thunderstorms, ice storms, tornadoes, lightning storms, flood storms, tropical storms, and hurricanes (just to name a few). Spiritually, there are only two types of storms: a "God" storm and a "You" storm. A God storm is a storm that has come into your life which God has orchestrated and allowed and He is going to see you through it. These types of storms were very prevalent when Jesus was training the disciples. Jesus wanted them to know the importance of spiritual authority. In one storm, he rebuked the wind and the waves and commanded peace to be still: in another storm, he defied the elements and walked on water. Jesus was training the disciples through hands-on illustrations and on-the-job training. In the Book of Acts it was God himself who orchestrated the double storm Paul was caught in. This storm was so severe it caused the ship to break into pieces. God had given Paul a word and a promise that everyone would live and make it to safety and he also gave him instructions for survival. Paul gave the instructions to those aboard and everyone survived. Many people became believers because of that experience. This teaches us that some storms we go through are not for us, but they are for others to witness the power of God working through us. A "you" storm is this simplest of them all; these are the storms that are caused and controlled by you. It's your obedience or disobedience that can stop or start these unnecessary storms. Jonah gave us a great example of a "you" storm. Jonah did not want to obey God; he boarded a ship headed in another direction, opposing what God said and a storm arose. The storm was so strong it troubled everything and everybody on the ship until they had no choice but to throw Jonah overboard. Immediately after he was thrown off the ship, everything calmed down. This teaches us that disobedience brings unnecessary storms. The storms often stop, and peace comes when we start obeying and doing the will of the Lord. It also teaches us to get rid of people in our lives who cause unnecessary chaos and confusion (throw them overboard). As Sons and Daughters of God, no storm is ever wasted; they are lessons to be learned. The next time you are faced with a storm, do a storm check; investigate whether it's a "God" storm or a "you" storm. (Psalm 107:29,89:9, Proverbs 10:25)

Day 18 Scriptures

Matthew 7:24-27

4 Therefore whosoever heareth these sayings of mine, and doeth them, I will liken him unto a wise man, which built his house upon a rock:25 And the rain descended, and the floods came, and the winds blew, and beat upon that house; and it fell not: for it was founded upon a rock.26 And every one that heareth these sayings of mine, and doeth them not, shall be likened unto a foolish man, which built his house upon the sand:27 And the rain descended, and the floods came, and the winds blew, and beat upon that house; and it fell: and great was the fall of it.

Pslam 17:29

29 He maketh the storm a calm, so that the waves thereof are still.

Pslam 89:9

12 The hearing ear, and the seeing eye, the Lord hath made even both of them.

Proverbs 10:25

25 As the whirlwind passeth, so is the wicked no more: but the righteous is an everlasting foundation.

Write it out

Journal Prompt:
Storm check! Is this a "God" storm or a "you" storm"

PHYSICALLY

Do you not know that your body is the temple of the Holy Spirit within you, whom you have from God? you are not your own, you were bought with a price. so glorify God in your body.
(1 Corinthians 6:19-20)

When an artist unveils a masterpiece, it is usually his or her most precious, preserved, piece of artwork. We are God's masterpiece. When He made us, He made us different from everything else that was made. He pulled out of Himself and made us in His image. Our bodies are a part of God's masterpiece and artwork. When we take care of our bodies, it shows that we honor the work of the Creator. We are so uniquely made that none of us are alike; even identical twins have something in them which makes them different from their other twin. God is a master craftsman who takes joy in His finished work. Caring for our bodies glorifies God; it's not His will that any of us should perish in sickness and disease, but prosper and be in good health, even in our very soul. (3 John 1:2). The way God looks at physical wellness is far different from man's perspective; man looks at the outside, God looks at the inside. The inside always has a way of showing up on the outside. Men's focus is usually on triceps, biceps, or maybe even a smaller pant/dress size, but God's focus is on the internal and not external. When we work on the inside, the outside somehow follows suit. God works from the inside out. God even made a promise to His chosen people in Exodus: if you all can just keep the inside pure and honor my laws, I will keep you from sickness and disease. Exodus 15:26…says it this way, "and if you listen carefully to the voice of the Lord your God and do what is right in his eyes, if you pay attention to his commandments and keep all his degrees, I will not bring on you any other diseases that I brought up on the Egyptian's I am the Lord who heals you.." God wants us to treat our bodies with proper nourishment, good self-care, rest, and respect. Although our bodies will eventually decay and perish, the Lord honors stewardship; He wants us to be good stewards over the bodies He has permitted us to live in here on earth.

Day 19
Self-care

The Devil has a secret weapon that he uses against so many believers, a weapon that often goes unnoticed, but it's very common. The name of this weapon is "busy." He keeps us so busy we don't have time to do the necessary things to live a balanced life. Being busy is not always being productive. Being so busy can also be a distraction and keep you from doing what really matters, especially if you're a person that has to wear multiple hats. We often get so lost in doing things for other people and going about our daily routine, we lose track of ourselves and forget about self-care. Self-care is not only when you attend to your physical and mental health, it's also soothing practices of comfort, balance, and peace. Caring for yourself deals with the real you: it penetrates to the core of who you really are. Simple things such as eating well, exercising, and getting proper rest are basic components of self-care and can significantly reduce anxiety and stress. Adding things such as journaling, picking up a hobby, taking time to hang out with friends, being adventurous, going on weekend trips, or basically carving out some me/personal time in your day to sit in silence and disconnect from everything around you is vital. When you do this, you can recharge, reboot, and reset your entire day and change your entire life. Jesus knew the importance of self-care. He would often leave the disciples and go away for solitude and personal prayer (Luke 5:16). There's only one person in the Bible that is referred to as his friend and that was Lazarus. The Bible says that Jesus would often retreat to Lazarus' house. We must take notes from Jesus and find a place for retreat. When you become mindful of your own limits and needs, you become aware of the need for self-care. Jesus even taught his disciples the importance of self-care in Mark 6:31-32; he made them eat and rest after a busy day. Self-reflection is the result of self-care. Take the time daily to invest in you; I assure you, the return will be well worth it. (Psalms 139:13-14, 1Corn. 6:19-20)

 ## Day 19 Scriptures

Luke 5:16
16 And he withdrew himself into the wilderness, and prayed.

Mark 6 :31-32
31 And he said unto them, Come ye yourselves apart into a desert place, and rest a while: for there were many coming and going, and they had no leisure so much as to eat.32 And they departed into a desert place by ship privately.

Psalms 139:13-14
13 For thou hast possessed my reins: thou hast covered me in my mother's womb.14 I will praise thee; for I am fearfully and wonderfully made: marvellous are thy works; and that my soul knoweth right well.

1 Corinthians 6 6:19-20
19 What? know ye not that your body is the temple of the Holy Ghost which is in you, which ye have of God, and ye are not your own?20 For ye are bought with a price: therefore glorify God in your body, and in your spirit, which are God's.

Write it out

What does self care look like for you?

Day 20
Get Uncomfortable

A few years ago on Facebook, I stumbled across an amazing fitness trainer by the name of Grover Neal. Grover created a group on Facebook called "Time to Get Fit." What made this group so different from other fitness groups is he stressed accountability and moving the body daily. Grover consistently posts new workout plans and different things to do to achieve your desired fitness goal. He often makes a statement I can never forget, and it always challenges me. He always tells the followers and those he trains, "It's time to get uncomfortable." This statement can be used in so many areas of our lives. Being comfortable does not bring change, it brings contentment. As the old saying goes, *"In order to get what you never got, you got to do what you've never done."* Gover challenges his followers to do new routines, new exercises, change their diets, or increase the number of set/reps in order to achieve greater results. I applied his technique to several areas of my life. I had to make myself uncomfortable and challenge myself so I could achieve a greater level of success.

Oftentimes in our lives, God will make things uncomfortable so we can embrace divine change. He told the prophet Jeremiah take a trip, I want you to go down to the Potter's House, tell me what you see. Jeremiah explains that he saw a potter working at the wheel and when the potter thought it was good, he tore it down and started it over until he made a pot pleasing to him. We're constantly on the potter's wheel. God is constantly molding, making, and shaping us into what he wants us to be and oftentimes, this molding and shaping is quite uncomfortable, but the results will bring success to our lives and glory to God. Getting uncomfortable challenges us to change. Change is never easy, but it's necessary. God made Abraham uncomfortable when he told him to leave his country and relatives. God was going to take him to a new land, bless him, make his name great, and make him a blessing to many others. That was indeed an uncomfortable challenge and change. (Gen. 12:1-3). There's a saying I read recently which caused me to understand the benefits of getting uncomfortable: "Great things never came from comfort zone's" (Roy T. Bennett) (Isaiah 43:19)

Day 20 Scriptures

Genesis 12:1-3

Now the Lord had said unto Abram, Get thee out of thy country, and from thy kindred, and from thy father's house, unto a land that I will shew thee:2 And I will make of thee a great nation, and I will bless thee, and make thy name great; and thou shalt be a blessing:3 And I will bless them that bless thee, and curse him that curseth thee: and in thee shall all families of the earth be blessed.

Isaiah 43:19

19 Behold, I will do a new thing; now it shall spring forth; shall ye not know it? I will even make a way in the wilderness, and rivers in the desert.

Write it out

Don't forget to write your day 20 reflections!

Day 21
Do something

Our physical well-being has a lot to do with living a life of wholeness and completeness. This will often require us to do as the Scripture says, forgetting those things which are behind us and pressing ahead toward the mark, a prize of a higher calling. To me, the "mark" and the "prize" mentioned in the scripture are those things we aspire to and desire out of life. Life is a risk and a gamble, but one worth taking: we have to choose whether to be complacent or move toward our goals and ambitions. It is our choices that influence our destiny. Choices reveal our options, our options present opportunities, and opportunities lead to opulence. 2 Kings chapter 7 records a story of four leprous men. Leprosy in the Bible was a dreadful disease and those who had it were considered unclean outcasts from society. They were not allowed to mingle with the rest of the community and had to live off whatever was given to them out of the kindness of others. In the story, the four lepers stayed at the entrance of the city gate during a severe famine in Samaria. To make matters worse, the enemy of Samaria was approaching the city, ready to take advantage of the misfortunate time and overtake the city. People were dying from the famine on the inside of the city, the enemies were approaching on the outside of the city, and the four lepers were stuck in the middle. It appeared to be a hopeless situation for them.

One day, they decided to explore their options and make a decision. They said, *"if we go in the city we will die because of famine and if we go to the camp of the enemy we may die as well, but why sit here and die? Let's get up and do something."* They chose to take a risk by going to the enemy's camp and see where their fate lie. To their surprise, they found that their enemies were gone, but the camps were intact. God had caused calamity, fear, and confusion to come upon the enemy's camp and they fled for their lives, leaving everything intact. The lepers were able to eat and collect the belongings and possessions left behind. They shared the information with others in the city and everything began to change for the better. Their decision to make a move did not just shift their future, but also those around them. These four lepers decided to get up and do something; they did not want to settle for what was going on around. They explored their options and those options led them to an opportunity for change. That change gave them opulence. The word opulence means wealth and financial gain. If these four lepers had decided to sit and settle, this story would have ended in a different way. Throughout life, we must explore options, take risks, make the choice to do something, and watch how God let's it work for your good. (Rom 8:28) (Psalms 119:133)

Day 21 Scriptures

Romans 8:28

28 And we know that all things work together for good to them that love God, to them who are the called according to his purpose.

Psalms 119:133

133 Order my steps in thy word: and let not any iniquity have dominion over me.

Write it out

What options are you exploring in your life right now?

Day 22
Ability

"If you have run with the footman, and they have wearied you, then how can you contend with horses? And if in the land of peace, in which you trusted, if they wearied you, then how will you do in the floodplain of Jordan?
(Jeremiah 12:5)

Knowing your ability can be extremely beneficial in this ever-changing world. Ability is the power of capability and the capacity to do or act physically, mentally, legally, morally, and financially. Ability is also related to your competence, level of activity, occupation, skill, training, and intelligence. Oftentimes, your ability can be limited, but it's good to know those limited abilities can be enhanced. When something lacks adequate power, strength, and physical or mental ability, it is considered a disability. When training the body to be physically healthy, and to reach a level of desired physical success, you must first start by knowing your current ability. No weightlifter starts off lifting 500 pounds; they must start based on their ability and build accordingly to achieve the ultimate goal. God has given us all an ability; this ability is a part of our personal destiny and life's purpose. Your abilities are often locked into your talent, skills, and even your hobbies. God entrusts us to enhance these abilities so that we can live a purpose-filled life.

The Gospel of Matthew chapter 25 verses 14-30 gives a great illustration of what God expects of us based on our abilities. Each man was given a talent based on his ability; those that took the talent and doubled it or enhanced it, received a reward and accolades from the master. The person that took it, hid it, and did nothing with it received correction and rebuke. It is our responsibility to enhance every gift, every talent, and every ability God has entrusted to us. Here are a few positive quotes to help and inspire you to enhance your ability so you can achieve success and fulfill your purpose. (1Peter 4:11) (Phil 4:13)

Ability is what you're capable of doing, motivation determines what you do, attitude determines how well you do it. (Lou Holts)

Personal power is the ability to take action. (Anthony Robbins)

Day 22
Scriptures

1 Peter 4:11
11 If any man speak, let him speak as the oracles of God; if any man minister, let him do it as of the ability which God giveth: that God in all things may be glorified through Jesus Christ, to whom be praise and dominion for ever and ever. Amen.

Philippians 4:13
13 I can do all things through Christ which strengtheneth me.

Write it out

Don't forget to write your day 22 reflections!

Day 23
Rest & Relief

The physical body is so uniquely made. God is truly the mastermind of craftsmanship. This is displayed when He made the complex body of man. We are made up of many cells, tissues, and organs. Every system of our body works in divine collaboration with each other. There are two things in life that work together to make our complex body operate in tip-top condition: rest and relief. Rest and relief are extremely vital to living a healthy life. Rest can be summed up as refreshing quiet and/or ease, mentally, spiritually, and physically. Rest often produces tranquility and calm. Rest reduces stress and improves your focus and your overall health. Rest is also a vital part of the healing process. Most of the time, our body is at rest when we are asleep. Sleep is so important because it enables the body to repair from an active day and prepare for the activities ahead. When we sleep, it causes the body to release hormones that slow breathing and relax muscles. During sleep, the blood pressure drops, and the heart takes a little break. Sleeping reduces inflammation and can assist the body in healing itself. Good sleep is the medicine we all need. Once the body receives adequate rest, it moves into a state of relief. Relief is alleviation, ease, and the science of deliverance through mental, physical, and emotional renewal. The Bible says during Creation, on the seventh day, God rested. If God rested, then surely, we should take a rest as well. Jesus often took time to rest and he also made the disciples implement rest in their daily routines. Relief is the automatic result of rest. Relief brings about a pleasing change, consolation, and comfort. This comfort begins to overwhelm you and happiness occurs. Learning to rest and achieving ultimate relief will sometimes require you to say no, change your diet, exercise, have daily quiet time, and stick to a sleep schedule. The results will be very beneficial: you will have sharper brain function and be in a better mood, have a healthy heart as well as achieve athletic success, and maintain healthy weight control. Love yourself enough to rest and enjoy relief. (Exodus 33:14 Matt.11:28-30)

Day 23 Scriptures

Exodus 33:14
14 And he said, My presence shall go with thee, and I will give thee rest.

Matthew 11:28-30
28 Come unto me, all ye that labour and are heavy laden, and I will give you rest. 29 Take my yoke upon you, and learn of me; for I am meek and lowly in heart: and ye shall find rest unto your souls. 30 For my yoke is easy, and my burden is light.

Write it out

How can I rest and find relief this week?

Day 24
Eat to live

"You are what you eat, so don't be fast, cheap, easy, or fake..." (Unknown)

I recently had a conversation with a dear friend and brother of mine who is a certified fitness trainer. I was sharing with him my goals, ambitions, and vision for how I desire my body to be and telling him the things I was doing in the gym. He commended me for them, but then he told me something that changed my whole perspective on building my dream body. He told me that bodies are built in the kitchen; what you eat plays a vital part in physical change. When we talk of living a life pleasing to God, we tend to ignore or forget that giving God glory also includes living a healthy life and being disciplined in our diet. 1 Corinthians 10:31, " so whether you eat or drink or whatever you do, do all to the glory of God..". God wants to be pleased with every area of our life, not just spiritually but physically as well. A poor diet could be a reflection of the relationship you have with yourself. Oftentimes when you are upset and displeased with yourself based on a bad decision or a bad experience, you will find yourself eating what we call "comfort foods." These foods may have very little to no nutritional value, but are pleasing to the pallet and the taste. Our relationship with food can mirror the relationship we have with life. The book of Daniel chapter 1 gives us a great example of the benefits of a good diet. Daniel and his three friends were captured by the Babylonians and were chosen to be servants in the King's Palace. They were told to eat of the king's royal food, however they chose to eat a healthy diet that consisted of raw, natural seeds, fruits, and vegetables. 10 days later, they were compared to the others who ate the king's royal food. Daniel and his companions were more mentally sharp and their physical bodies, as well as complexion, were healthier than the others. Eating to live influences us to be more aware of the foods we consume so we can live healthier, stronger, and happier lives. Eating is a major part of our life, so if we eat well, we can live well.

Day 24 Scriptures

1 Corinthians 10:31

13 Whether therefore ye eat, or drink, or whatsoever ye do, do all to the glory of God.

Daniel 1:8-9

8 But Daniel purposed in his heart that he would not defile himself with the portion of the king's meat, nor with the wine which he drank: therefore he requested of the prince of the eunuchs that he might not defile himself. 9 Now God had brought Daniel into favour and tender love with the prince of the eunuchs.

How can you improve your diet and eating habits?

FINANCIALLY

"And God is able to make all grace abound toward you, that you always have all sufficiency in all things, may abound to every good work"
(2 Corinthians 9:8)

The word sufficiency stands out to me heavily when it comes to this scripture and understanding finances. The word sufficient sums up the characteristics of financial stability and freedom in a very beautiful way. It means having enough to obtain the things necessary for a specific purpose. When we understand that all sufficiency comes from God the Father then down to His children, our financial dependency becomes easy. We realize that He is the ultimate source. Philippians 4:19 states, "...my God shall supply all my needs according to his riches in glory by Christ Jesus..". Understanding that God is your supplier and ultimate source is very important when it comes to financial stability, freedom, and abundance. Once we understand that God is our source, we must exemplify the power of giving. Luke 6:38 "..give and it shall be given to you in good measure, pressed down, shaken together and running over shall men and give to your bosom. For with the same measure that you give all it shall be measured to you again...". Giving to God lets him know you can trust him for more. Giving to others lets God know that you're not selfish, and just as he has given to you, you're willing to share with others. Our giving is connected to our stewardship. Stewardship is being faithful and wise concerning the things that God has charged to us; this is where the financial discipline comes into play. Living within our means and margins and not squandering or wasting things that God has trusted us honors God and will most likely lead to a debt-free life. Taking on financial obligations that are hard to keep up with and buying things beyond our ability to pay is what causes financial downfalls. Psalms 37:21, "...the wicked borrow and pay not again." Proverbs 22:7, "..the rich ruled over the poor and the borrower is the servant to the lender."

Controlling our spending is a major key to financial freedom and living a financially stress-free life. Connecting with people who are financially literate, wise, and competent can really influence financial success. Seeking financial wisdom is always a plus when it comes to advancing financially. Proverbs 23:23 says, "through wisdom is in the house builded; and by understanding it is established: and by knowledge shell the chambers be filled with all precious and pleasant riches..". When we seek God as our source, live a life of giving, manage those things that God has charged and given us as a good steward, and seek wisdom of financial management, development, and growth, we will be able to move up and forward as debt-free believers. We will also become the financial leaders God has predestined us to be.

Day 25
Sell, Pay, Live

Not all miracles in the Bible deal with sick bodies or are demon-possessed people; there are a few miracles in the Bible I consider economic, or financial. A life on Earth requires us to constantly live with and consider debt. How well we manage our debt can lead to financial stability, but there are times when the unexpected comes and managing our debt can become difficult. Second Kings chapter 4 gives an interesting miracle about a woman who was faced with a debt after the death of her husband. In the story, we see that the woman was in distress because the creditors were coming to take her sons as slaves to satisfy the debt of her late husband. She went to the prophet for help and he gave her instructions that would change her life. First, he asked her, "What is in your house," or in other words, what resources do you have to work with? She said to him, "All I have is a little bit of oil," understanding that in the Bible days, oil had multiple uses and was vital for financial revenue. Second, he told her to borrow as many vessels as she could, then pour the oil into the borrowed vessels until there were no more vessels. This lets us know that God can work with the little we have left. The widow had to put the work in as well. After she poured all the vessels full, He gave her another set of instructions that totally changed and turned her situation around. He told her to sell the oil, pay her debts, and live off the rest. If we understand this concept, and the miracle that worked for the widow woman, it will also work for us. Find out what resources we have around us with potential to bring in necessary or extra revenue. Pay off all of our debts from money earned and then, make it a habit to live off of the rest/ what's left. In other words, live within your means. Live a life of meaning, enjoy life, enjoy the things you have acquired.

Things to take note of:
God will bless those who make money the honest way.
God wants us to pay our debts.
God wants us to be wise and have a plan on how we will spend money.
(Proverbs 10:4, 21:20)

Day 25 Scriptures

Proverbs 10:4
4 He becometh poor that dealeth with a slack hand: but the hand of the diligent maketh rich.

Proverbs 21:20
20 There is treasure to be desired and oil in the dwelling of the wise; but a foolish man spendeth it up.

Write it out

What resources do you have in your home that can increase your wealth?

Day 26
The Mouth & The Money

The mouth is a very important part of the body. Naturally, it is the mouth we use for eating, whereby we gain nutrition. It is also what we use for verbalization and communication. Spiritually, our mouth can draw positive and negative things to us. The Bible says we are justified or condemned by what we speak (Matt. 12:37). It also says we can speak blessings and curses from our mouth (James 3:10). Every day, we must monitor the manuscript of our mouth. In the Gospel of Matthew, chapter 17:22-27 there is an interesting story. Peter was one of Jesus' key disciples. I guess one would say that Peter was the head, or the lead disciple, however Peter always had a problem with his mouth. He was always the one to speak before thinking, or to speak out of his emotions. Even after the crucifixion of Jesus, it was Peter who spoke from his mouth in denial of Jesus. His mouth was always getting him into trouble. On this particular day, there were a group of tax collectors who wanted to question Peter about Jesus paying taxes to the temple. Instead of Peter using wisdom to tell them to ask Jesus for themselves, he quickly responded "yes" without consulting Jesus. When he got back to Jesus, knowing what was done, Jesus corrected him nicely and gave him instructions on how to get the money needed to pay the debt. Since Peter was a fisherman, Jesus used what he was familiar with. He told him, go to the sea, cast a hook, and take the fish that comes up first, and when you have opened its mouth, you will find a piece of money, take that and give it to them for me and you. (Vrs 27). There are several interesting facts about this miracle. First, note how Jesus told Peter to use his skill to get what he needed. We must understand that our craft and the work of our hands were given to us to bring revenue and financial gain. Second, Jesus told Peter to look in the mouth of the fish that he caught. He did not say look behind the fence and look in the belly, he said the mouth. This was relating the lesson to the very thing that got Peter in trouble. Oftentimes, God will turn our mistakes into miracles. The third thing to note is that when God blesses us financially, he always gives us more than enough. He told Peter that the money in the fish's mouth would be enough to pay my taxes, and yours. Peter's mouth got him into debt, but the mouth of a fish got him out of debt. Start speaking positive affirmations and declarations over your finances and use some mouth-to-mouth resuscitation to bring money into every area of your life. (Prov. 18:20, 20:15)

Up & Forward: 30 Day Devotional

 Day 26 Scriptures

Matthew 12:37
37 For by thy words thou shalt be justified, and by thy words thou shalt be condemned.

James 3:10
35 And the same day, when the even was come, he saith unto them, Let us pass over unto the other side.

Proverbs 18:20
20 A man's belly shall be satisfied with the fruit of his mouth; and with the increase of his lips shall he be filled.

Proverbs 20:15
15 There is gold, and a multitude of rubies: but the lips of knowledge are a precious jewel.

Write it out

Use the journal section to create positive affirmations for finance.

Day 27
Don't give up to soon

Dealing with finances can often be a frustrating thing. It seems like as soon as you get one debt paid, another debt arises. The adversary (the devil) will even plant seeds of negative thoughts in your mind to make it seem as if everybody is doing a little bit better than you. This can make you feel frustrated, depressed, and like you want to give up. It is during those moments we have to find hope and strength to encourage ourselves, as well as hang around positive influences. Go in prayer and ask God for wisdom as well as a strategy to lead you into a place of financial deliverance. In the Bible, there was a man who happened to be a skilled fisherman who came in contact with Jesus. Not knowing the magnitude of who Jesus really was, the fishermen allowed him to sit in his boat and talk and teach to a multitude of people. The fisherman was so frustrated because he had been fishing all night and caught nothing. He had even washed his nets, symbolizing that they were done for the day. However, Jesus gave some instructions and told the fisherman: get in your boat, launch out in the deep, and let your nets down. The fisherman replied, nevertheless, at your word. He let his net down, but to his surprise, there were so many fish the net was about to break. He had to call in for help and those who helped had their boats filled with fish as well. This fisherman became Jesus' number one disciple, Peter. I just think; if Peter would have given up and not believed in the instructions or strategies of Jesus, his outcome would not have been positive. His blessing was so big that he had enough to share with others. God always gives us more than what we ask for. The Scripture says He will do exceedingly and abundantly above all we can ask or think.

(Ephesians 3:20). Even in hard times, you may even feel like Peter and start washing your personal net, thinking you're done; it's over. But remember, all you need is a word from the Lord; whether it comes from prayer and meditation, a Bible verse, or even a song. Develop a "nevertheless" attitude and keep trying because after a while, like Peter, your net will be filled with abundance. Don't give up too soon, launch out into the deep: He will give you the instructions you need to get the abundance you've been seeking. (Psalms 55:22, Proverbs 3:5, Galatians 6:9)

 **Day 27 Scriptures**

Ephesians 3:20
20 Now unto him that is able to do exceeding abundantly above all that we ask or think, according to the power that worketh in us,

Psalms 55:22
22 Cast thy burden upon the Lord, and he shall sustain thee: he shall never suffer the righteous to be moved.

Proverbs 3:5
5 Trust in the Lord with all thine heart; and lean not unto thine own understanding.

Galatians 6:9
9 And let us not be weary in well doing: for in due season we shall reap, if we faint not.

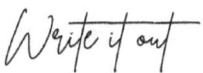

In what ways can you cultivate a "nevertheless" attitude to keep trying?

Day 28
The Power of Process

Process is defined as a systematic series of actions directed to some end. Process is vital when it comes to achieving success in every area of our lives, especially financially. I heard a seasoned, well-known preacher give advice to some younger preachers. He told them, "I know you all admire the major platforms and the large stage, but never forget, it's the small steps that step up to the large stage." Every detail in the process leads to a greater purpose. The Bible even tells us not to despise small beginnings; small beginnings can have major endings. Better is the end of a thing than the beginning (Zechariah 4:10). The life of Joseph in the Bible is a life of process. Joseph was one of Egypt's most influential men, but it didn't happen easily. He went through a painful process that I like to call the pit, the prison and the Palace. Joseph was a man of favor; his father favored him, but his brothers envied him. Because his brothers despised him, they threw him into a pit and contemplated killing him, but they ended up selling him into slavery. While in slavery, he gained the favor of his master and had rule over everything in the master's house. Because of a lie and a false accusation, Joseph found himself in prison, but while in prison, God favored him again. He began to have leadership in the prison. Despite the prison location, his gifting led him to the palace where he was favored again, but this time by the king. Joseph was given a position of authority and influence. Please note, throughout this entire painful process, the Bible says repeatedly that the "Lord was with him." This lets us know that throughout every dark process of our life, when the Lord is with you, He will favor you and get you through it. Like Joseph, you may have had a pit experience dealing with your family and generational dysfunctions. Although it may have been negative, understand that it's a part of your destiny to find a way to turn it into fuel for your future. Know it can be used for a greater cause. You may have even had a prison-like experience; been misunderstood, lied too, stepped on, or even falsely accused, but God has a way of turning that into stepping stones for your success. No experience, bad or good, is ever wasted; understand that it's a part of the process. Joseph led Egypt into its greatest economic time; the things he learned from the pit and the prison caused him to prosper in the palace. As the story ends, years later when Joseph finally meets up with his brothers, the same ones who envied him and almost killed him, he did not become bitter. He forgave them and made a powerful statement to them. He said, you meant it for evil but God meant it for good. Nothing big happens overnight. Remember small hinges open big doors; don't ignore the process. (Jeremiah 29:11,Ecclesiastes 8:6,Rom 8:28)

Day 28 Scriptures

Zechariah 4:10
10 For who hath despised the day of small things? for they shall rejoice, and shall see the plummet in the hand of Zerubbabel with those seven; they are the eyes of the Lord, which run to and fro through the whole earth.

Jeremiah 29:11
11 For I know the thoughts that I think toward you, saith the Lord, thoughts of peace, and not of evil, to give you an expected end.

Ecclesiastes 8:6
6 Because to every purpose there is time and judgment, therefore the misery of man is great upon him.

Romans 8:28
28 And we know that all things work together for good to them that love God, to them who are the called according to his purpose.

Don't forget to write your day 28 reflections!

Day 29
How to Deal with Dirty People

What a wonderful world it would be if everyone celebrated each other's physical and financial success? The upside of living a financially secure life is reaching success and new heights because of goals, ambitions, and hard work. The downside of financial success is dealing with others who are jealous and envious. Envy is called the green monster because it can destroy lives, both personally and professionally. The University of Cincinnati School of Business did a study concerning envy in the workplace. Its findings determined that envy can be extremely detrimental to employees and employers. I've heard people say when you're doing well, lookout for hate. A major determining factor when dealing with jealousy, hate, or even envy, is how you respond.

We cannot control how people view us or even feel about us, but we can control our response. Rely on positive energy and never lose focus so you will remain successful. The Bible gives us an example of this in Genesis chapter 26. We find Isaac, the son of Abraham, had God's favor and blessings on his life. Everything Isaac did succeeded. Isaac was such a success that the neighboring king envied him (vs.14). In the Bible, wells were rare and symbolized success. Those that dug the wells intended to inhabit or live in the area for a while. The Bible states that every time Isaac's herdsmen dug wells, water sprang up. Finding water requires patience and skill, but these men were lucky; every time their shovel hit dirt, water sprang up. The neighboring herdsmen noticed this and began to quarrel, arguing over the wells and even stopping / plugging up the wells by throwing dirt in them. Each name of the well was significant: the first well was named

"Esek"and it meant "to quarrel" or "to argue." The second well was named "Sitnah," it means "hatred"or "hostility." The third well was named "Rehoboth," which means "spacious," or "enough room." To plug a person's well could be ruinous to the owner and calls for serious aggression, often leading to war. Instead of Isaac retaliating, he told his herdsman to keep moving and keep digging. When the neighboring herdsmen saw they were unstoppable and determined to keep digging, they left them alone and did not contend with them. When they dug the third well Rehoboth, Isaac was determined not to let the dirt stop him or his herdsmen. He instructed them to keep digging and to keep moving because every time they dug, water sprang up. He focused on his productivity, and not his problem. This teaches us, don't argue or quarrel with those that may throw dirt, or envy, or even hate; because of your productivity or success, stay in motion, keep it moving, up and forward. Not only will you hit water every time, God will make room (Rehoboth) for you at the top. (Psalm 37:1-3, Proverbs 14:30)

Day 29 Scriptures

Genesis 26:14
14 For he had possession of flocks, and possession of herds, and great store of servants: and the Philistines envied him.

Psalm 37:1-3
Fret not thyself because of evildoers, neither be thou envious against the workers of iniquity.2 For they shall soon be cut down like the grass, and wither as the green herb.3 Trust in the Lord, and do good; so shalt thou dwell in the land, and verily thou shalt be fed.

Proverbs 14:30
6 Because to every purpose there is time and judgment, therefore the misery of man is great upon him.

How do you respond to difficult people/situations?

Day 30
Finances, Favor & Good Health

Beloved I pray that you prosper in all things and be in health just as your soul prospers.
(3 John 1:3)

Finances, favor, and good health are what I consider the trinity for successful living. We truly understand that finances are a vital part of living; to be financially secure is everyone's prayer and desire. Education, wisdom, knowledge, and discipline are just a few tangible characteristics which assist with financial success and security. When the tangible things connect with the spiritual things, we can reach unknown financial heights. Favor is a spiritual component that goes far beyond money. I like to say when money ends, favor begins. It's God's favor that causes the unexplainable to happen in our lives. Luke 2:52 says "..and Jesus grew in wisdom and structure in favor with God and man..". If Jesus had to grow in favor, then so should we. Favor means to show preference and/or something done or granted out of goodwill. When favor is prevalent in your life, it brings assistance, benefits, respect, support, admiration, grace, and kindness. The Bible is filled with examples of people who received and lived with favor. Noah found favor with God, Joseph experienced favor because the Lord was with him, Israel found favor with the Egyptian's, Moses had favor in the sight of God, Ruth found favor with Boaz; these are just to name a few. Favor is often unexplainable; you just know it's there. Finances and favor are indeed a good combination, however neither would be any good if you did not have good health to enjoy it. An ailing body can rob anyone of enjoying the pleasures of life. To be in good health is an ultimate gift that shouldn't be taken for granted. Practicing good health is our responsibility and a part of stewardship. God often favors us when we care for our bodies and see our bodies as His temple and dwelling place. "Everything is permissible for me but I will not be mastered by anything therefore honor God with your body," (1Corinthians 6:12,20). Exercising discipline in our bodies coupled with favor and finances, will cause us to live a whole, complete life and find success in every area; spiritually, mentally, physically, and financially. (Deut 8:18, Psalms 30:5, 91:16)

Up & Forward: 30 Day Devotional

# Day 30 Scriptures

Luke 2:52
52 And Jesus increased in wisdom and stature, and in favour with God and man.

1 Corinthians 6:12, 20
12 All things are lawful unto me, but all things are not expedient: all things are lawful for me, but I will not be brought under the power of any20 For ye are bought with a price: therefore glorify God in your body, and in your spirit, which are God's.

Deuteronomy 8:18
18 But thou shalt remember the Lord thy God: for it is he that giveth thee power to get wealth, that he may establish his covenant which he sware unto thy fathers, as it is this day

Psalms 30:5
5 For his anger endureth but a moment; in his favour is life: weeping may endure for a night, but joy cometh in the morning.

Psalms 91:16
16 With long life will I satisfy him, and shew him my salvation.

Write it out
Don't forget to write your day 30 reflections!

Bonus Journaling Section

Day 01
Break the Shell

Thoughts, reflections & Prayers

Day 02 — Essential Needs (Mentally)

What are your day 2 thoughts?

Up & Forward: 30 Day Devotional

Up & FWD Mentally — **Day 03** *You're Able*

Write your day 3 prayer below

Day 04
Up & FWD Mentally — *Needful Mindfulness*

How can you practice mindfulness in your life today?

Up & Forward: 30 Day Devotional

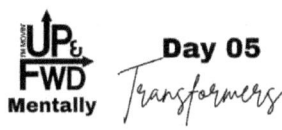

Day 05
Transformers

What do you ned God to transform in your life?

Day 06

Musical Medication

What songs assist in modifying your mood and refocusing your mind?

Day 07: Feelings are not Facts

Up & FWD Emotionally

What are you feeling today?

Up & Forward: 30 Day Devotional

Up & Forward: 30 Day Devotional

Day 08
Emotionally Emotional Enemy

In what areas do you need more self control?

Up & Forward: 30 Day Devotional

Day 09
Altered Anger

How can you respond to anger in a healthy way today?

Up & Forward: 30 Day Devotional

Day 10
Fruit Filled

What seeds have I sown and what fruit do I see?

Up & Forward: 30 Day Devotional

Day 11
Almost

I almost...but I am so glad God...

Up & Forward: 30 Day Devotional

Day 12
Just Do it

Today I am committed to doing...

Day 13: The Struggle is Real

Up & FWD Spiritually

What are you wrestling with?

Up & Forward: 30 Day Devotional

Day 14
Spiritually: Command, Control, Create

Dear God help me to control..create... and command...,

Day 15
Spiritually: The Odds are in your Favor

What are you seeking God's direction for?

Up & Forward: 30 Day Devotional

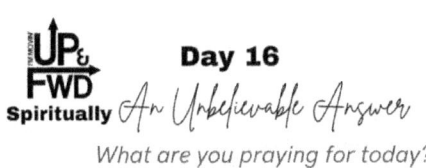

Day 16
Spiritually An Unbelievable Answer

What are you praying for today?

Day 17: It's not what it Looks Like

UP & FWD Spiritually

What was your eye opening experience?

Up & Forward: 30 Day Devotional

Day 18
Storm 101

Storm check! Is this a "God" storm or a "you" storm?

Day 19
Self-Care

What are you seeking God's direction for?

Physically

Day 20
Get Uncomfortable

What does self care look like for you?

Up & Forward: 30 Day Devotional

Day 21

Do Something

What options are you exploring in your life right now?

Day 22
Ability

Which positive quote sticks out to you and why?

Up & Forward: 30 Day Devotional

Day 23
Rest & Relief

How can you find rest and relief this week?

Day 24
Eat to Live

How can you improve your diet and eating habits?

Up & Forward: 30 Day Devotional

Up & Forward: 30 Day Devotional

Day 25 — Financially
Sell, Pay, Live

What resources do you have in your home that can increase your wealth?

Day 26
Financially — The Mouth & The Money

What are your reflections from day 26?

Up & Forward: 30 Day Devotional

Day 27
Up & FWD Financially! Don't give up too Soon

In what ways can you cultivate a "nevertheless" attitude to keep trying?

Up & Forward: 30 Day Devotional

Day 28
Financially — The Power of Process

What are you praying for today?

Day 29
Financially: How to deal with Dirty People

How do you respond to difficult people/ situations?

Up & Forward: 30 Day Devotional

Day 30
Finances, Favor & God Health

How has the up & forward devotional helped you?

Up & Forward: 30 Day Devotional

ABOUT THE AUTHOR

Dwight Follins is a native of Jacksonville Florida, he was educated in the Duval county public school system, and a graduate of Sandalwood Senior high school class of 1992. At a young age Dwight received many awards and accomplishments in ministry, music and arts. For twenty years he was employed with the Duval Country Public schools as a community Based Instructor (CBI) for students with disabilities. In 1995 Dwight became the worship leader and assistant minister of music at Alexander Temple Community Church in Jacksonville Florida. In 2005 being lead of the Lord Sr. Bishop Donna McCollors installed him as a licensed Elder and co-pastor. As the Lord showed Elder Follins continuous favor in ministry he became well sought out revivalist, and workshop facilitator. In 2012 with much prayer, he embarked upon full time ministry, this decision opened numerous doors of ministry and opportunity. Today Elder Follins is the founder of several successful prayer clinics in Jacksonville FL, Atlanta Ga, and Philadelphia PA. In 2017 Elder Follins released his 1st book, a guided prayer Journal entitled *"A Minute & A Moment"*. Elder Follins ministry can be experienced on social media hosting Mid-Day/Noon Day prayer with participants nationally and internationally, reaching an audience of 5 to 10,000 views weekly. It's Elder Follins prayer and heartfelt desire that those who experience his ministry receive hope, help, and healing.